RAISING
CHASTE
CATHOLIC MEN

Practical Advice, Mom to Mom

LEILA MILLER

Catechism quotations are taken from *Catechism of the Catholic Church* (2nd ed.). Washington, DC: Libreria Editrice Vaticana-United States Conference of Catholic Bishops, © 2000.

Scripture quotations are taken from the New Revised Standard Version, Catholic Edition, copyright 1989, 1993, Division of Christian Education of the National Council of Churches of Christ in the United States of America. Used by permission. All rights reserved.

Cover design by Connie Rossini and Beth Pack. Cover photo, "Stopping in to visit Jesus," by Beth Pack.

LCB Publishing
4427 E. Blanche Drive
Phoenix, Arizona 85032
raisingchastecatholicmen@gmail.com

Ordering Information:
Quantity sales. Special discounts are available on quantity purchases by moms' groups, parishes, associations, and others. For details, contact the publisher at the address above.

Raising Chaste Catholic Men/Leila Miller. —1st ed.
ISBN 978-0-9979893-0-4

To my parents, Dr. Farouk and Mary Habra,
who chose life for me twice, in birth and in baptism.
I cannot thank them enough for all they have done for me.

~

To my beloved cousin and friend, Michelle Jean Habra,
who left us for her true Home on April 13, 2015.
Her passion for the moral formation
of her children rivaled my own.

~

And to the Blessed Mother,
who took me under her mantle when I was little,
waited patiently for me when I strayed,
and has never let go of my hand since I returned to the Church.
She teaches us all how to conform our lives to her Divine Son:
"Do whatever He tells you."

Contents

Acknowledgments

The Good Lord knows I couldn't do any writing, much less write an entire book, without lots of help and encouragement!

First, I pour out my undying love and gratitude to my husband Dean, who does more in one day that I do in a week, and who always picks up the slack when I let things drop. I specifically want to thank him for not getting mad when I typed and typed on a glowing computer into the wee hours of the morning in the same room where he was trying to sleep (usually with a blindfold and occasionally with earplugs).

To my wonderful children, who have humored me... er, cheered me on through my blogging adventures and now as I attempt my first book. Oh, and thanks for staying chaste! Without that, this book would not have been possible. Heh heh.

To the following incredible ladies who oh-so-patiently and kindly brought this work, logistically, to fruition:

Connie Rossini, seasoned self-published author, who took all the pieces I gave her and shaped it into a real, live book. No mean feat.

JoAnna Wahlund, for her proofreading and edits. She is one of the few people on the planet whom I trust for accuracy in theology *and* grammar.

Beth Pack, for shooting the cover photo before I had even written a book to go with it, and for lending one of her own adorable hooligans as its star.

To my blog readers, Facebook friends, and my local "little Catholic bubble" — the Phoenix Catholic community — for all the support and friendship you have given me as I gestated and birthed my firstborn book baby. You guys are the best.

And finally, I'd like to express my deepest gratitude to my own beloved shepherd, Bishop Thomas J. Olmsted, for taking the crisis of manhood seriously by writing *Into The Breach*, the apostolic exhortation to Catholic men, which inspired much of this book.

Leila Miller
Feast of St. Monica, 2016

Introduction

On the Feast of the Archangels, September 29, 2015, Phoenix Bishop Thomas J. Olmsted promulgated *Into the Breach: An Apostolic Exhortation to Catholic Men.*[1] As the mother of many sons, one particular line jumped out at me and grabbed me by the lapels:

> Imagine standing before the throne of God on judgment day, where the great saints of ages past, who themselves dealt with preeminent sins in their own day, will say to each other, "We dealt with the trouble of lust in our day, but those 21st century men! These happy few battled the beast up close!"

The sexual sins are the sins of our day. There is no denying it, and there is no denying that our men and boys struggle mightily to remain chaste and retain their purity in a world designed to incite lust and drag them down to the dark pit of hell.

Dramatic? Nope, it's just reality. Sin is real, hell is real, the temptation surrounding our sons is real. Far from suggesting that we become apathetic or despairing, I am incredibly hopeful and confident that our boys can avoid the sins of unchastity and thrive as healthy, unaddicted, free men of God, ready to lead their families as devout and honorable husbands and fathers one day or lead the faithful as holy priests. This is not a pipe dream, as I see it happening all around me.

Over the years, several Catholic mothers have come to me, asking for help; specifically, they wanted me to write something on raising up "good Catholic men" or "real Catholic men" in this corrosive culture. Recently, I received two message requests in two days from two amazing Catholic women whom I greatly admire (ahem, Amy and Katie), and it suddenly hit me that it was time to start writing.

The level of worry out there is high, and if you are reading this, you are probably at least a little bit concerned yourself. One great mom of littles, Beth Pack (who shot the cover photo for this book), told me, "This is the thing I am most worried about with my kids. Porn and sexual sins destroy lives."

Catholic mothers feel inadequate, helpless, and even hopeless about the onslaught that their boys will face as they leave the safety of their homes and face the outside world. By the grace of God, I was spared that particular worry. When my husband, Dean, and I were hit with the truth and beauty of human sexuality and conformed our lives to it (six years and three children into our marriage), my confidence soared. This makes sense! This is clear! This works! This is truth!

Perhaps my confidence was naïve, but so far it has been justified: My oldest three boys have grown through adolescence, and all three have embraced chastity.

This is not a pat on my own back. It's a humble and joyful acknowledgement that God is sovereign. He is bigger than this culture, and we need to have faith and hope and trust that His promises are real and transformative. Divine grace is not fairy dust or some imaginary, nebulous, "feel good" construct. It is real, and it is powerful. It is the very life of God within us, and when we have it, we can act with heroic virtue — an ultimately attractive thing for boys and men, whose desire for heroism is hard-wired into them by their Creator.

I want you to hear in this book that I am no different from you, and your boys are no different from mine. You *can* do this. Do not fear, and do not be anxious! If you are living in accordance with Catholic teaching and fully assenting to the sexual moral law, it is possible to raise your sons to be chaste and free, not slaves to sin. Remember that God has adequately equipped you to be an effective and fruitful parent. He has given you all the tools you need, and with His grace, you can bring up your boys to be who He made them to be.

This book will be a practical guide of what that journey might entail, and how to prepare your sons to "battle the beast up close."

Onward!

What This Book Is Not

Okay my friends, before we dive in, I want to tell you what this book is *not*.

This is not a general Catholic parenting book. Others have done that and done it well.

This is not a book about teaching manners, or social graces, or any of life's niceties (of which I am very much in favor, by the way).

This is not a book about how to raise Catholic gentleman per se, although I have said more times than I can count, "I will raise Catholic gentlemen if it kills me!" But while not about raising gentlemen generally, this book or any book promoting male chastity will touch upon it, since chastity and gentlemanliness coincide.

This is not a book on the basics of Catholic teaching. Although this is a Catholic book, both the discussion and advice herein *presuppose* that you are already a practicing, faithful Catholic and that your children are being raised in the Catholic Faith. It *presupposes* that you are teaching your children about God the Father, Son, and Holy Spirit, about the Incarnation of

Jesus Christ, His teachings, His miracles, His Mother Mary, His Church and the sacraments He established, His Passion, atoning death on the Cross, and bodily Resurrection, the Communion of Saints, the absolute necessity of Scripture and prayer, etc.

You should be reading "Jesus, prayer, sacraments" between every line. If you aren't doing that part, the advice here will not be effective. I also pray that you have at least an elemental understanding of the truth and meaning of human sexuality and Theology of the Body, but if not, check the Appendix for resources.

This is not a book about raising *daughters* in a pornified culture, although my husband and I have raised two chaste daughters, both grown and married now, and there are many points from this book that can apply to girls as well. However, considering the current crisis of manhood *and* the number of Catholic moms who have asked me specifically about raising good Catholic men, I am making boys the focus of this volume.

This is not a book that represents, denies, or usurps the father's role in the life of a boy/teen/young man. The role of a father in a young man's life cannot be overestimated. Fathers and other male role models are crucial for forming boys into good men. However, the only people who have asked me to write on this subject are women, and it's something I can approach only from a woman's perspective (for obvious biological reasons). My husband is not a writer, so his book on this subject will never materialize, but he's fully on board with all that I am writing here (thank you, Honey!).

This is not an exhaustive treatment of the subject matter, not by a long shot. So very much more can and should be said, and yet I know that my readers are busy moms with very little time to spend on a book. I wanted to make this as short and sweet (and practical) as possible.

This is not a book of new revelation or ideas. You may find yourself nodding your head as you read along. You likely could have written this book yourself, because what is contained herein is pretty much common sense. It's important to have reinforcement and encouragement, though, from other moms who understand. These words will not blow you away as if you are learning something brand new, but they will confirm you in what you are already doing or want to be doing. They will remind you that you don't have to be reactionary or have freak-outs simply because the world around you and your family has gone mad. It's okay to be living in this culture because God knew it would be this way, and He placed you here with a job to do. This book is simply to reinforce the sanity and truth that will already ring familiar in your soul, making you a better Christian witness in a wounded, confused world.

This book is not a statement that I have somehow figured it all out, and that I am an expert on the subject of raising chaste young men. I am an expert on exactly nothing. I have no credentials other than being the mother of eight children, six of them sons. In raising those sons, I have noticed that some things have worked for us and could probably work for others.

This book is not a guarantee against subsequent moral failures by me or my sons. There is no way to predict if my sons will continue to stay on the straight and narrow path. Virtue, otherwise known as moral excellence, is a habit that has to be cultivated; at the time of this writing, my boys are in the habit of the virtue of chastity. Free will, however, is a funny and fearsome thing. God gave us the precious gift of free will — without which we cannot *choose* to love and are left as merely robots or slaves — and it's the one thing He will not touch. It's ours alone, and until the moment of our death, we are free to choose good or evil. At any moment, my mature, older sons could choose to go off the rails, and there is also no guarantee that my three younger sons, still in grade school, will use their free will wisely. However, even if they or I should fall, I believe that what is written here has value.

This book is not a scholarly work, not a book of research, not a treatise of deep philosophy or theology. This book is the equivalent of one Catholic mom sitting down over a cup of tea with another mom in my kitchen, to talk informally but quite seriously about navigating this culture with your boys' morality and chastity intact — and to give you the confidence you need to do just that.

So, what is this book? It's just a casual conversation between friends.

Let's get started....

Chapter One
The Basics

I lay down the foundational principles below with three assumptions: you love God, you serve God, and you teach your children to do the same.

In other words, I assume I am preaching to the mothers in the Catholic choir.

Read this well: Your children are not stupid. They know very well if you take your faith seriously or if you are picking and choosing which parts of the Catholic Faith or the moral law to obey — and they will interpret that to mean that they can, too.

If you are picking and choosing, you have lost your moral authority to teach your children obedience to Christ, as your children can easily sniff out a lack of integrity, and if you have lost your moral authority with your children by dissenting from Church teaching, my advice here will be ineffective.

Now that we have established your love of God, faithfulness to the Magisterium, and acceptance of the entire Deposit of Faith, let's start with general, foundational principles that we can put into practice.

In looking back over a quarter-century of parenting and asking my older children for their thoughts, I have identified three keys to raising solid, morally responsible kids in a culture of relativism:

1. Moral formation is the top priority.
2. What I teach must make sense.
3. Nothing is off limits for discussion.

Let's take them one at a time:

#1 — Moral formation is the top priority

When I say "top priority," I mean that with every fiber of my being, and my kids know this. It really doesn't matter what else I do as a parent, because if I fail in the kids' moral formation, I not only fail them, but I also fail society and God.

I have a suspicion that the average American parent no longer places "moral formation" at the top of their priority list. It seems to me that "academic/career/financial success" or "popularity" have taken the lead, followed by a general philosophy of "Whatever makes my child happy!"

Oy, vey.

If we don't raise our children to be morally upright, first and foremost, then we miss the point of parenthood entirely. There are enough financially successful, popular, and "happy" villains in the world already. What we lack are *saints!* My children know, because I say it often enough, that I don't care if they are "happy." That's not my job. *True* happiness comes from the peace and joy of a life well lived. *Lasting* happiness is our goal, not temporary, giddy pleasures that cannot be sustained and leave us bored, miserable, and looking for the next temporary high.

The moral, honorable man has a joy that no one can steal and a peace that surpasses all understanding, as Christ promised. That's what we are going for here, my friends. That's what we want for our children, and we mustn't be shy in telling them so.

Now, it goes without saying that a child can be properly formed and still go wildly off the rails due to misuse of that pesky gift of free will. But woe to me if my child crashes into the ditch because I never placed and secured the rails in the first place.

#2 — Our beliefs and principles need to make logical sense

Please understand this! We live in an age of non-stop information. Not knowledge, not wisdom, just information. All of these conflicting bits and chunks of data are competing with us for the very souls of our children. If we don't explain to our children why our Catholic Faith is logical, coherent, cohesive, consistent, and beautiful, they will have no reason to stick with it when the rest of the world tells them it's stupid, superstitious, oppressive, irrelevant, and evil.

Young people really do want to transcend the noise, chaos, and sin to find the straight path. They really do want their world to make sense, and our job is to show them that it does.

To that end, here is what we must *never* say to our inquisitive children:

"I have no idea why the Church is against [fill in the blank], or why we believe [fill in the blank]. You just need to follow the rules!"

No, no, no, *no*! What we say instead is:

"Well, Honey, I am not sure exactly why the Church teaches that, but I am going to find out and get right back to you. The Church always has a good answer."

That's when you open your *Catechism of the Catholic Church*, check reliable Catholic websites on the Internet (try Catholic Answers at catholic.com) or send an email to me at raisingchastecatholicmen@gmail.com if all else fails. Resources to help you are everywhere. I have watched the first four of my eight children reach adulthood. Each of the four has not only kept the faith personally, but also publicly, even in a hostile culture — even while at non-Catholic schools and large state universities where the majority of their peers do not hold, understand, or even respect their Catholic worldview.

They have kept their faith through hardships and challenges because they see the truth of it. It makes sense. It especially makes sense when contrasted to the literal nonsense and relativism that surrounds them. They are able to see in their non-believing, non-practicing peers the consequences of living life in the "nonsense" versus living life as a faithful Catholic.

They certainly are not saints, and they have friends of all stripes and beliefs, but, by having the proper moral formation, they are able to make sense of the world, make sense of sin (their own and others'), and make sense of suffering. All the world, all of human activity, has a context for them, and *it makes sense.*

#3 — Nothing is off limits for discussion

And I do mean nothing. Sex, drugs, death, hell, crime, whatever. Age appropriate, of course, but nothing is forbidden.

My kids know that whatever they ask me will be answered. I am approachable, and I want them coming to me before they even think about going to anyone else.

A few years ago, my middle-schooler came to me with a one-two punch of shocking questions regarding things he had heard from his peers, things I could never repeat here. My face stayed relaxed, I met his gaze without betraying my alarm and horror, and I calmly gave him the explanations and information he needed.

When he and I finished our talk, he left the conversation relieved and satisfied, and so did I. The straight talk we had was informed by our faith, which *made sense to him* (principle #2), and the discussion was a catalyst for *deeper moral formation* (principle #1).

See how seamlessly that works?

It sounds easy, doesn't it? And it *is* easy and uncomplicated, unless parents get caught in the starting gate, too spooked to go forward, specifically on the subject of sex. It troubles me when even devout Catholic parents say that they avoid such discussions, or don't have them at all. They tell me they don't know what to say. I say, *too bad.* You have to do it. That's your job. They are your children, and you need to take them seriously, look them in the eye, and tell them the truth. They want to hear it from you, and they will absorb your wisdom on these matters. Don't let them down.

If you are still unsure if you can do it, it might motivate you to know that the Church herself is very clear on parents' **obligation** and **duty** to teach their children about sex. The

Pontifical Council for the Family wrote an entire document on the subject in 1995, *The Truth and Meaning of Human Sexuality: Guidelines for Education Within the Family.*[2] I discovered this important document after a string of good Catholic mothers confessed to me that they could not or would not speak to their children (some already teens and adults) about sex. I was completely baffled, disturbed, and concerned. If these incredible Catholic moms weren't telling their children the truth about sex in a culture designed to destroy faith and devour souls, then we're in big trouble!

The Vatican document calls parents to something higher than they might be aware. I printed the whole thing out, took a yellow highlighter in hand, and looked specifically for the words "obligation" and "duty." I was not disappointed by what I found. Here's a sampling (the following eight paragraphs are direct quotes; emphases in italics are in the original, and emphases in bold are mine):

> In many cases parents have given up their **duty** in this field or agreed to delegate it to others, because of the difficulty and their own lack of preparation. (#1)

> The Church has always affirmed that parents have the **duty** and the right to be the first and the principal educators of their children. (#5)

> Parents who carry out their own right and **duty** to form their children for chastity can be certain that they are helping them in turn to build stable and united families, thus anticipating, insofar as this is possible, the joys of paradise.... (#33)

> As husband and wife who have become "one flesh" through the bond of marriage, they share the **duty** to edu-

cate their children through willing collaboration nourished by vigorous mutual dialogue.... (#37)

The Holy Father John Paul II reaffirms this in *Familiaris Consortio*: "The right and **duty** of parents to give education is *essential*, since it is connected with the transmission of human life; it is *original and primary* with regard to the educational role of others, on account of the uniqueness of the loving relationship between parents and children; and it is *irreplaceable and inalienable*, and therefore incapable of being entirely delegated to others or usurped by others", except in the case, as mentioned at the beginning, of physical or psychological impossibility. (#41)

If in fact parents do not give adequate formation in chastity, they are failing in their precise **duty**. (#44)

In particular, with regard to use of television, the Holy Father specified: "... Evasion of this **duty** is made easy by the presence of television and of printed materials in the home...." (#56)

Parents in particular have the **duty** to let their children know about the mysteries of human life, because the family "is, in fact, the best environment to accomplish the **obligation** of securing a gradual education in sexual life...." (#64)

The Church understands and the document explicitly confirms that our duty as parents is more difficult today than it was in generations past. Why? Because before the sexual revolution and its corrosive effects on society and innocence, the greater culture, both secular and religious, actually supported families in the ideal, norm, and expectation of chastity. The document acknowledges that parents today cannot even rely on the past examples of parents and grandparents, as they did not have to face and counter what we parents have to face and counter today. Just like young men, we parents, also, are "battling the beast up close." This is a whole new ballgame.

In addition to stressing parents' rights, responsibilities, and sacred duties, the Church stresses her own obligations:

> [T]he Church holds that it is her **duty** to give parents back confidence in their own capabilities and help them to carry out their task. (#47)

In other words, you are not alone! The Church is here to help, with an abundance of teachings, wisdom, reason, moral theology, and the power of the sacraments. Use what the Church is offering you as a parent. Christ established the Church to teach and sanctify the faithful on our journey through life to eternity. Trust what she knows and what she can offer.

Now, let's get specific and practical. What type of parent/child relationship would make it easier to fulfill these sensitive and sometimes awkward duties? I'm glad you asked....

Chapter Two
Be His Parent *and* His Friend

We've all heard it: "Children need a parent, not a friend!" I had always agreed with this saying, even repeated it loudly myself, and yet I began to wonder: Are parenting and friendship mutually exclusive? When I reflected on my own experiences as a mother, I concluded that they are not. I began to recognize that, like all human relationships, the parent-child relationship is deeper than any slogan.

I believe we can find a balance. I want to be, on an appropriate level, a true friend to my children. For years, I was embarrassed to admit that, fearful of being mistaken for one of the "cool" moms who make me cringe, the ones who are desperate for their kids to "like" them and who never quite grow up themselves. Clearly there is a danger in being too familiar with your child. Crossing the line into oversharing, dumping your emotional baggage, or expecting a child to take on the role of an adult or partner is inappropriate and damaging. That kind of familiarity smacks of desperation, and the children of these needy and/or "cool" moms are often a mess themselves. Many eventually want very little to do with their mothers. Such familiarity is more an abdication of the parental role than a real friendship.

However, I want (and blessedly have) the kind of healthy, warm familiarity that finds even my high school sons home with the family on most weekend nights, piled onto our bed or sprawled out on the couch next to it as if they were still little kids. I don't mind their innocence and closeness. They are not strange, socially inept, or insecure, they just like hanging out with their parents and siblings, watching a movie or shooting the breeze on a Friday night. We've worked to cultivate that as parents, and I won't discourage it. Soon enough, as I know all too well already, these moments will end and they will be off to college and an adult life. While the active parenting will be done then, the friendship will remain.

goals

What kind of friendship between parent and child, then, is appropriate and desired? I like this definition of friendship that I found at CatholicCulture.org:[3]

> Reciprocal love. In philosophical terms a friend is a person whom one knows and loves well and by whom one is known and loved for virtuous reasons. The biblical notion of friendship, in the New Testament, adds the feature of total selflessness after the example of Jesus Christ, whose love was generous, forgiving, and sought only the welfare of those whom he loved. The sharing of confidences is also part of the biblical understanding of friendship (John 15:15).

Friendship, then, is a special affection, a close relationship marked by enjoyment of each other's company, sharing things in common, having inside jokes, and a general feeling that "we like one another." True Christian friendship is grounded in a love of virtue, never a connivance in vice.

Parenting, which we discussed in the previous chapter, is the formation (character and moral) and education of one's children, requiring an exercise of God-given authority and a ton of confidence (fake it till you make it, ladies!). We are accountable before God Almighty for our parenting, which is our sacred vocational duty.

Maintaining a harmony between parenting and friendship is the challenge we face. Let's talk specifically about our sons.

My personal ideal, not always realized, is to be a firm and authoritative (not authoritarian) parent, and also a trustworthy, loyal, and cheerful friend. In my non-expert, non-researched opinion based on personal trial and error, parenting and friendship can coexist, *so long as the parenting part stays firmly in place and takes priority if there is a conflict between the two.*

Strong, sound parenting helps facilitate a good friendship with your child. You cannot really have fun and enjoy the company of a son whom you have not parented well. When a parent is loathe to firmly parent a child for fear of making the child "feel bad," or hoping to spare the child negative emotions, the child becomes ill-behaved, whiny, disobedient, entitled, manipulative, and overall unlikable! When I have allowed myself to be emotionally manipulated by a child, when I didn't want to "hurt" him with boundaries and accountability (or when I was too lazy for follow-through), my relationship with that child became strained, distant, and even hostile. Friendship at that point was impossible, as we really did not like one another. These were the hardest times in my parenting, as I think all moms can understand. We women are relational by nature, and it stings terribly when the mother-child relationship is wounded.

So, no matter how much you might dislike it, be a firm parent first and foremost. If you fear that your child will resent or hate you, consider the following story, which is one of the most gleeful memories I have:

My oldest son must have been about 12 years old, and he would readily admit that he was not an easy child to raise. He was in the swimming pool with some of the younger boys and I was sitting outside watching. He was on a tear of complaints, lamenting about whatever guideline or standard we were imposing on him, when he finally, nastily spat out the words: "You are the only mother I know who cares about their child's character!" What he thought would be a poison-laced dagger in my heart was in fact the cause of my instant joy! A huge smile broke out on my face, and I giddily responded with, "Yesssss! That is the best thing you could have ever said to me! Thank you for confirming that I am on the right track!" I danced around and laughed. Meanwhile, my son became mute and sulky, recognizing that he stepped right into that one, but I couldn't wipe the smile off my face for hours. Today, he and I are able to laugh about it, and he's glad that I was "that mom."

We want our children to understand that their character development and spiritual welfare are the most important things to us as parents, don't we? Isn't that the way that they actually know that we love them?

Consider another incident, this time with my second son, which confirms that standing firm is exactly what our children want from us, despite what they say. When he was a young teen, he had been manipulating me time and again about an issue. I wanted my boy to be "happy" and not mad at me, so I keep caving to his demands. This caving made him bolder and more obnoxious, until finally I'd had it. I put my foot down, asserted my authority, and yanked all his privileges. He knew I meant business. I'll never forget when that angry scowl turned into a gentle grin of approval and he said, "Now, that is some good parenting, Mom." Not sarcastic, not rude — the kid meant it! It was humbling to know that my previous attempts to placate him had actually been earning me his disrespect. He didn't like the consequences he now had, but he was actually thrilled that I was acting like a parent, not a pushover.

Which brings me back to the friendship part. It was only because we are friends that my son could be open and honest with me in saying what he did with a touch of humor. He didn't want me to fail in this endeavor of parenting, and because we are friends, he "had my number" and could call me on it. He encouraged me when I needed it. And when the proper order of authority was restored, the friendship rebounded as well.

You don't want to fall into the trap of being afraid of your children and their reactions when you lay down the law, but you don't want your children to be afraid of you, either. To that end, we must do what was not the norm in previous generations: We must apologize easily and openly admit our mistakes. Some parents go the other way and do not want to show any of their weaknesses, vulnerabilities, or humanity to their children. But then the parent becomes impenetrable to the child, and, frankly, unlovable. The lovability and affection between a mother and her son is crucial to parenting and formation, as it eases uncomfortable situations, facilitates tricky conversations, and makes it more likely that your child will really hear you when you speak and come to you when he has a problem.

A few months ago, I had the following text exchange with my (then) 15-year-old son, which illustrates what can happen when a parent is also a friend; he came to me as a friend, and asked me, explicitly, to be a stronger parent:

"I'm gonna be honest. I'm not doing very well in French or Chemistry."

"What does that mean? And how diligently are you studying?"

"That's the problem. I want to do well, but I'm too lazy. I need to be accounted for."

"Okay, then we need to do that, and you can't fight us. We are old and tired. But we can hold you accountable."

"I need that."

Boom! I'm going to count that as a parenting win, even indirectly. He made us more accountable in making him more accountable. Before we had a friendship, this son never would have confessed to bad grades on his own, and there is a respect between parent and child that might not have been there if the "friend" part of the equation had not been cultivated.

You might be thinking that if we had simply been harder on this child as he grew up, he would not be in this predicament. He has given me permission to share that we had an extremely difficult time with him for many years. In fact, we doubled-down on the "parenting" back then, neglecting the "friend" part for much of his young life. It was awful. We were awful. And there was no real affection, no trust, no enjoying each other's company.

We finally let go of the need for control and parental domination. We relaxed and remembered that he is beloved by and made in the image of his heavenly Father, and that no two children are the same. We began to enjoy his company and recognize his unique gifts. He came back "into the fold" of the family, and even found a more loving embrace from his siblings, who had also been put off by years of bad behavior. When the fighting lessened, everyone was happier and more relaxed. And yes, in backing off a bit, we let him experience the natural consequences of own his actions or inactions, part of which were poor grades.

When I was a younger mother, receiving that kind of text might have worried me or made me angry. As it stands, it didn't bring up any negative emotions towards my son. In reading his words, I felt like this young man understands the need for the virtues of diligence and industriousness, and is asking, on his own, for help to achieve it. The will is in place, an appropriate parent-child friendship is in place, and that's something we can work with!

Now that we've explored the general disposition needed to help us have that healthy relationship with our sons, let's get back to their training in chastity and how that all begins....

Chapter Three
When They Are Little

Most of what you need to know about chastity and your sons' early years can be summed up in two sentences:

1. Respect the latency period.
2. Don't freak out about stuff.

The latency period, or what St. John Paul II called the "years of innocence," spans from about age 5 to puberty and is easy enough to understand. From *The Truth and Meaning of Human Sexuality*:

> This period of tranquility and serenity must never be disturbed by unnecessary information about sex. During those years, before any physical sexual development is evident, it is normal for the child's interests to turn to other aspects of life…. So as not to disturb this important natural phase of growth, parents will recognize that prudent formation in chaste love during this period should be indirect, in preparation for puberty, when direct information will be necessary. [#78]

Our Church tells us to respect the latency period of children, which would ideally last until the child hits adolescence;
however, we live in a society that does not respect a child's
innocence. In fact, the world around us seeks to destroy innocence, by design. The educational establishment, advertisers,
books, movies, television, and video games — all push to sex-
ualize children at a young age. In fact, entities like SIECUS and
Planned Parenthood, which have routine access to public
schools, believe that children should be immersed in secular,
relativistic sex education from birth. The materials used for
those even as young as kindergarten are sexually explicit and
incredibly disturbing. Start a Google search and see what I
mean, but don't say I didn't warn you.

What to do when the latency period is violated? We must
step in. Again, from the Church:

> A further problem arises when children receive premature
> sex information from the mass media or from their peers
> who have been led astray or received premature sex educa-
> tion. In this case, parents will have to begin to give carefully
> limited sexual information, usually to correct immoral and
> erroneous information or to control obscene language.
> [#84]

Dean and I have learned that precisely when to speak to
our young children about sex and how detailed to get will be
different for every child we have. For example, even as I sat
down to write this chapter this morning, I received the following text from the fourth grade teachers at my son's public
charter school:

> Fourth Grade: The Birds and the Bees seem to be of inter-
> est in the fourth grade! It has come to our attention that
> how babies are made is a topic of conversation. You may

want to touch base with your child to see if he or she has been "educated" by a peer.

And so, this evening my husband and I will be gently questioning our 9-year-old to see if we must "begin to give carefully limited sexual information" as the Church has said.

Another of our children, a daughter who was unusually precocious and curious, came with questions at the tender age of six. She was not satisfied with the usual, age-appropriate answers to "Where do babies come from?" and kept pushing, pushing, pushing ("But *how* does God make those babies?" "How does the baby *get* in the mommy's tummy?"). She was relentless, and so I finally gave her some basic biology — at which point she stopped asking, probably regretting her questions! I directed her not to discuss any of this with peers at her small orthodox Catholic school, as I could just imagine the fallout from conscientious parents learning that their own little ones' latency periods had been disturbed prematurely! I myself was concerned by the whole situation, wondering if I had ruined my own daughter by telling too much too soon. I am grateful to report that this child, now a grown wife and mother, remained committed to her faith and to chastity even after her early introduction to reproductive biology.

Another one of our children looked as if he might skate right on into adolescence itself without asking *any* questions, and so there came a day when Dean and I decided that he needed to hear from us before he heard from his peers. It was not so much disturbing his latency period as it was a prudential judgment that he was old enough and "in the world" enough to necessitate the discussion. We considered it a pre-emptive strike against what would have been a peer-driven, secular education had we not stepped in. In fact, we learned at about the same time that he had already begun to hear some talk about sex but had not let on.

In our home, "the talk" consists of the same-sex parent (the boys with Dean, the girls with me) sitting down with the child and a book titled, *The Joyful Mysteries of Life* — what we affectionately call "the little orange book." It's an unassuming, unadorned, thin volume, written by a French couple, Catherine and Bernard Scherrer, and translated into (sometimes awkward) English. The book contains an endorsement by Alfonso Cardinal López Trujillo, then the President of the Pontifical Council for the Family, who in his forward describes it as an excellent companion to *The Truth and Meaning of Human Sexuality*. You would want to read through the book first, to decide which, if any, parts to leave out.

At first I thought this little book would be too old-fashioned or hokey for today's more sophisticated kids, but I have been continually surprised by the positive responses we've gotten from the children. The last son who read it with Dean was our then-fifth grader, a "cool" kid who has it all together. Instead of making fun of the language and approach, this child would ask eagerly every night, "Is it time to read the next chapter yet, Dad?"

I wonder if we sometimes underestimate the power of the truth and how much our seemingly coolest, most independent sons want to hear about human sexuality from their parents, not their peers.

There are, unfortunately, two topics that will undoubtedly confront our children in some form or another before they have left the latency period: Abortion and LGBT issues (homosexuality, gay "marriage," transgenderism). These cultural tsunamis are so pervasive that they're going to come up and they must be dealt with.

Explaining abortion to a young child is an awful, horrifying thing to do, and I hate it every single time. My kids start to hear the word "abortion" fairly young, as we are quite active in the pro-life movement. Prayers to end abortion abound both in our parish, our kids' Catholic schools, and at the prayer vigils and rosaries in front of local abortion clinics. At a certain point, I have to explain what abortion is.

Think about that. How does a *mother* explain abortion to her own *child?* But it must be done, gently, clearly. "Sometimes mommies or daddies don't want their babies and they pay a doctor to take the baby out too soon." Obviously, this is simplistic and not the full range of scenarios, but it's bad enough.

So far, every child has had the same reaction. Disbelief, confusion, denial, horror.

How could anyone do that? Who doesn't love little babies? Who forces a mom to do that? How could a mom ever do that to her baby? Why would a doctor do that?

They really get the evil of it. You don't have to paint a picture or get graphic. Children are naturally pro-life, and the idea of someone deliberately killing a child in his mother's womb is so foreign to small children as to be absurd, nonsensical, insane. Their little minds sense the disorder immediately, and reject it.

It does feel like I'm taking their innocence by telling them the terrible truth of it. After all, once a child understands that our nation not only allows but celebrates the murder of other small children — the ones nestled in their mothers' wombs, just as they or their beloved siblings had been so recently nestled — how can they not be affected to their core?

After they experience that initial shock, don't forget to teach the mercy of God. Remind your child how much God loves all children and takes good care of the ones that have been lost in this way. And remind him to pray for the mommies, daddies, and doctors involved, that they might repent of this terrible sin, because God and those little babies want to see them all in Heaven one day. Explain how many people have changed their hearts on this issue and have gone on to be good men and women who fight against abortion now, similar to the way that St. Paul used to assent to the murder of Christians but went on to become one of the greatest Christians of all!

More recently, gay "marriage," transgenderism, and "gender fluidity" have stormed onto the scene and become unavoidable. What were not even issues when my first few children were born are now everywhere, even in children's programming. How can we explain all of this to them without going into details they should not hear? Again, by keeping it simple. If a child comes to you and says that he's heard of people "changing" from male to female, or that he's seen two men kissing, you might just say, "Wow, they must be very confused! That's so sad, and let's pray for them so that they aren't confused anymore!"

Or, if they ask about two men being "married," you might simply say, "Nope, boys can't marry boys," just like we adults have done for millennia when little ones innocently talk about marrying their friends or their same-sex parent. If an older child says, "But two men or two women are allowed to get married in America now," you simply remind the child that what is legal is not always right, and that courts and judges can be, and often have been, horribly wrong. And as your child gets older, you will teach him about the truth and meaning of marriage (see Chapter Five).

Now let's get to the second point to remember when they are little: Don't freak out about stuff.

Catholic mothers tend to worry, worry, worry, even when we shouldn't. This worry is counterproductive. We worry about the safety of the world, the decline of the culture, the seemingly bleak future that awaits our children and grandchildren. For those macro worries, we must heed the words of Pope Benedict XVI, who reminds us that we were made for this moment, and we are meant to be here on this planet right now: *"the sacrament of the present moment"*

> Dear friends, may no adversity paralyze you. Be afraid neither of the world, nor of the future, nor of your weakness. The Lord has allowed you to live in this moment of history so that, by your faith, his name will continue to resound throughout the world.

Mothers also worry about the little things. Every little thing, thousands of them, all the ways we could ruin our children or how they could ruin themselves. And yet, Jesus commands us not to worry even in the micro, asking, "Can any of you by worrying add a single moment to your life-span?" (Mt 6:27). No, we cannot. Leave worry behind, and replace it with trust.

Let's look at some specifics and get practical:

When a boy is a baby or toddler, he is likely going to touch himself and explore his genitals. This does not mean that he will become a compulsive masturbator, so relax. It's what little boys do. Boys like their penises. Some boys like their penises more than others, but you needn't be alarmed about it.

So, how do you handle it? Some boys only need to hear once or twice that "We don't play with our penis" or, cheerfully, "That's not a toy!" or my favorite as they get older, "Uh, that's not a handle!" — something I still say to my teens who routinely and unconsciously "adjust" themselves. It's become a bit of a joke, and I recommend a lighthearted attitude. Here's something I just this minute said to a youngster (and say often to all of them, who scratch and "reposition" no matter how old they get): "Get your hand out of your pants!" It's said firmly, but with a touch of good humor. They get it. And then I move along without dwelling on it or worrying about it. It's really not a big deal.

In fact, little boy bits are so ubiquitous in our male-heavy home that even our kitchen table has not been safe from a brush with small genitals belonging to clamoring, climbing toddlers who would frequently present themselves naked to dinner! "Get your private parts off the table, please, and go get dressed!" We still laugh about it (and I'm guessing you all just made a mental note not to eat at our house).

Now, you may not agree with our earthy way of speaking and relating, and that's okay. I support parents' rights to direct and speak to their children as they feel called — and that might look more reverent or decorous than in our home — as long as the necessary conversations are happening and innocent little boys are not shamed or made to feel dirty as they are being redirected. Whether you do your redirecting and virtue training with utmost reverence or with earthy good humor is your choice, as long as you do it.

By the way, I personally don't have a big emotional investment in whether or not other parents use proper, clinical words for their children's anatomy. Our kids know the technical names for their genitals, but we also call them "private parts" to get the "private" point across as well.

We are about to dive into a real irony. We Catholics do not want to have these difficult sex-related conversations with our small children in the first place. We want them to be children. We want them to keep their innocence and enjoy normal childhood relationships and development without everything being sexualized. And yet, it is Catholics who are accused, time and again, of being "obsessed with sex." Before we talk about adolescence and our teens, let's survey the cultural context and ground ourselves in the proper perspective....

Chapter Four

The Two Big Accusations

T wo charges are thrown against the Church so often and so reflexively that we must teach our children how to respond to them — and that means we must first know how to respond to them ourselves.

"The Church is Obsessed With Sex!"

If you speak to secularists at any length, or even to Christians who have wandered far from the virtue of chastity, you will hear the accusation constantly: "The Catholic Church is obsessed with sex!"

This silly charge is so pervasive and unquestioned that even many Catholics accept it as a given, and yet the claim is a head-scratcher to any reasonable observer, or anyone who grew up Catholic in America.

I went to Mass every Sunday growing up in the 1970s and '80s, and I don't recall ever hearing a homily about sex — not once. Today the topic might be more prevalent in some parishes due to the cultural shifts and crises, but even now it cannot even be said to be excessive, much less obsessive.

For those Catholics who make the claim that the Church is obsessed with sex, I'm guessing that they draw their views primarily or exclusively from media opinion, anti-Catholic teachers or professors, the entertainment industry, and/or secular friends, but not from their experiences in a parish, a look at the *Catechism of the Catholic Church*, or an investigation into Church documents.

Anyone who's lived in both the secular world and the Catholic world (as I have, pre- and post-reversion) knows that it is the Church's accusers who are, in fact, obsessed with sex. It's actually wearying. Sex seems to be all they think about and want to talk about, and they command and coerce the rest of us to think about it and talk about it, too. All.day.long.

Can anyone plausibly deny it?

There is raunchy, ever-more-explicit TV and cable sex; ubiquitous, graphic movie sex; infinite hours of dark, depraved internet porn sex; taxpayer-funded Planned Parenthood "sexperts" teaching our kids about oral sex, anal sex, group sex, masturbatory sex, homosexual sex, and making slick video tutorials for young people about the "skills needed" to navigate hook-up sex; non-stop testimonies about the goodness of homosexual sex; dating sites for casual and adulterous sex; sex in commerce and advertising (can't they just sell us the burger?); clothing that sexualizes little girls; explicit sexual lyrics in music; sex in music videos; simulated sex as dancing; sexting, sex tapes, girls and boys gone wild about sex, sex, sex, sex, sex! And even on my blog, commenters have proclaimed, quite seriously, that they COULD NOT LIVE without sex!

I think it's all a bit … *obsessive.*

And then we have the Catholic Church, plodding along through human history, saying the same thing about sex that she always has. She is a teacher and a mother, and she is *responding* to the culture's errors, *reminding* an amnesiac world what sex and marriage are all about.

The Church, after all, has taught the truth about human sexuality and the virtue of chastity for over 2,000 years, along with the rest of the moral truths and virtues, which do not and will not change. Chastity just happens to be the virtue that today's sex-obsessed culture neither appreciates nor approves, but that's an indictment of the culture, not the virtue.

Marriage is a holy institution established by God, and sex, a privilege of marriage, is a one-flesh union of man and woman rooted in biology and ordered toward the good of the spouses, of the children created, and of society at large. Nothing new here, just the same ancient, beautiful, non-frantic, non-obsessive truth taught by the Church (sometimes even too timidly) for millennia.

As opposed to this timeless truth, the sexual progressives of our day are pushing a fad, working hard to fashion a new sexual paradigm where anything goes (between "consenting adults," of course!) and there are no moral judgments. The frenzied campaign is on, full-speed, to change our understanding of the very nature, meaning, and use of human sexuality. The Church's opponents want to redefine marriage and family to mean things they have never meant and can never mean, and they don't want anyone to tell them no. They are making incredible headway, and they are so close to their goal that they can taste it. But they remain frustrated. Something is keeping them from guilt-free, genital carte blanche.

The one thing standing in their way?

The Church. That's all. No generals, no armies, nothing. Just Holy Mother Church, speaking the same old truths she has spoken for twenty centuries and will speak for twenty centuries more, or until no one is left on earth to hear her. The Catholic Church is the one voice lovingly, carefully, firmly proclaiming, whether anyone listens or not, that sex has a meaning and purpose that cannot be discarded without violating our human dignity. Even when certain members of the Church violate her teaching on human sexuality, including some of the very clergy sworn to holiness, the evil fallout and devastation wreaked upon the innocent is not a *negation of* but rather an excruciating *confirmation of* the moral law and the good of chastity.

Despite the utterly predictable, unwavering teachings of the Church, her opponents are often violently emotional in their quest to change her mind, silence her voice, or run her out of existence. Though they would like to claim an oppressor/victim model here, it's really more like a classic parent/teen showdown: "Give me my way and let me do what I want or I will scream at you and call you obscene names and tell you you are power-hungry, irrelevant, out-of-touch, full of sin yourself, and just plain mean!"

And the Church, as a good mother does, looks on her children with love and concern, even sadness, but stays steadfast, consistent, and confident. The rules of life don't change. Truth does not change. Love does not change.

As the sex-obsessed voices get louder and angrier, the Church has tried to raise her voice above the din, but not because of any obsession. In fact, as far as I can tell, no one in the Church really enjoys constantly addressing the sexual morass in which we find ourselves (if only it would just go away!), but we have to speak loudly and clearly for the sake of a very confused generation. Because responding with love and truth to the prevailing sins of each age is pretty much the Church's job description, and it's what we can expect her to do from now until, well, eternity. That's not obsessive, it's just faithful.

All reasonable people can understand this, including teens. Each adolescent or teen sees the culture around him. He sees sex and porn and objectification shoved in his face every day from every angle. With his own experience of the culture and a correct understanding of the Church's role, fielding the "Church is obsessed with sex" question won't be the most difficult challenge your child will face.

"The Church is Imposing Its Views!"

There is, however, another and more difficult accusation that will come to your children: "The Catholic Church has no right to impose its views on the world!"

The charge is so common now that most lukewarm Catholics accept it and most serious Catholics ignore it. But it's important that our children be able to see the landscape clearly so they aren't swayed by the sheer volume and frequency of charge.

Let's get our bearings by making some distinctions.

On some issues, the left would be correct about "not imposing Catholic beliefs." Those issues and beliefs that we may not "impose" are the ones that are specifically Catholic.

If, for example, we Catholics were working to force people, by law, to attend Mass, to access the sacraments, to profess the Marian Doctrines, or to abstain from meat on Fridays during Lent, our critics would be justified. We cannot impose points of the Creed, the unique tenets of our Catholic Faith, on others.

But then there is the universal moral law, what is also called the Natural Law (not to be confused with physical science/"laws of nature"). The moral law is for all people, and all people are accountable to the moral law. These are issues of human flourishing, of virtue vs. vice, good acts vs. evil acts, and they apply to everyone in all times and cultures and places. These universal truths are accessible by the light of human reason alone (no divine revelation required).

Abortion, euthanasia, slavery, human reproductive trafficking, rape, murder, theft, lying, cheating, marriage as conjugal union, the primary rights of parents and the family -- these things and more fall under the umbrella of the universal moral law, which is binding on all men.

Knowledge of the universality of the moral law is as old as mankind; it was philosophized about by the pagans in ancient times and has undergirded every major world religion since. Our own nation's founding principles were predicated on a belief in Natural Law ("Laws of Nature and of Nature's God" as the *Declaration of Independence* called it), and Natural Law was the basis of the Reverend Martin Luther King, Jr.'s arguments during the civil rights movement. He profoundly understood that the laws of men must correspond with God's law, as he explains in his famous "Letter From a Birmingham Jail" (1963):

> [T]here are two types of laws: just and unjust. I would be the first to advocate obeying just laws. One has not only a legal but a moral responsibility to obey just laws. Conversely, one has a moral responsibility to disobey unjust laws. I

would agree with St. Augustine that "an unjust law is no law at all."

Now, what is the difference between the two? How does one determine whether a law is just or unjust? A just law is a man-made code that squares with **the moral law or the law of God**. An unjust law is a code that is out of harmony with the moral law. To put it in the terms of St. Thomas Aquinas: An unjust law is a human law that is not rooted in **eternal law and natural law**. [emphases mine]

MLK understood what millennia of intellects, philosophers, statesmen, and saints have known, but which our own recent generations have utterly forgotten. I myself had never explicitly heard of the Natural Law until I was in my early 40s! Once it was explained to me, many things became clear.

If you are confused as to which topics are uniquely Catholic versus which topics are universal to all, there is a way to test it: You will find secularists and atheists who are against legal abortion (check secularprolife.org, for example), and you might even know some personally. You will also find secularists and atheists who believe in natural marriage — maybe your agnostic Uncle Al, or just check the atheist regimes around the world, whose heterosexual-only marriage laws obviously cannot be based on any religious tenets. What you will never find, however, are "Secularists for the Eucharist" or "Atheists for the Primacy of the Pope" or "Non-Believers for Mandatory Baptism." In other words, you will find non-religious folks everywhere who adhere the moral law, but none who adhere to the Nicene Creed.

Now, not every point of the moral law must or even should be enforced by civil law, but the biggies for humanity and society — such as human life itself, such as natural marriage, such as rights of conscience — must be protected in law for the common good.

Still with me? Okay!

Let's go ahead and define our term: What does "impose" actually mean?

When I Googled the word "impose," this was the first definition that popped up, so let's use it for our discussion:

> im ·pose
>
> /im'pōz/
>
> verb
>
> [To] Force (something unwelcome or unfamiliar) to be accepted or put in place.

Let's use gay "marriage" as our example, here. If you followed the campaign for gay "marriage" in America and the massive, pull-out-all-the-stops push for its acceptance that culminated in a Supreme Court decision wiping out all state laws protecting natural marriage, something should immediately jump out at you when you evaluate that definition. Do you see it?

Just in case it's too obvious to see, let's break it down....

Marriage as union between male and female has been a reality (a non-controversy, a given) not only for the entire history of America, but essentially for the history of all mankind. I often refer to the historically accurate words of Hillary Clinton on the subject (shortly before her historical knowledge somehow "evolved" along with the political winds), when she states her commitment to:

> ...the fundamental bedrock principle that [marriage] exists between a man and a woman going back into the mists of history, as one of the founding foundational institutions of

history and humanity and civilization, and that its primary, principal role during those millennia has been the raising and socializing of children for the society in which they are to become adults.[4]

Bam! Yes, this!

Until about two minutes ago, historically speaking, this basic understanding of the inherent heterosexuality of marriage *was the status quo.*

A bride and a groom (sexual complementarity) are needed for a marriage = status quo.

Enter the gay "marriage" movement, with its advocates working very, very hard to change the basic understanding of marriage. In other words, the gay "marriage" movement was trying with all its might to change the forever-standing status quo.

When a movement or group comes in and labors to replace what exists with something new that it demands, that is called *imposition.* It's *imposing.* The gay "marriage" advocates (and not the Church!) have actually been imposing their new view of marriage upon society.

Let's refer back to the definition above and plug in words to test it: The gay "marriage" movement has **forced (something unwelcome or unfamiliar) to be accepted or put in place**.

That fits.

And the force for acceptance has been powerful, as it was legally imposed from the top down. Meaning, the clamor and cry for the redefining of marriage did not grow upward from the American people as the 1960s-era civil rights movement did, but was instigated by secular elites and "progressives," led by lawyers and judges and professors and politicians. Their aim was to displace society's status quo (heterosexual) understanding of marriage, which had always been comfortable and quite acceptable to the people.

The truth is that all the movement, all the force, all the pressure, all the demands "to accept or put in place something unwelcome or unfamiliar" came from someone and somewhere, but it was not from the Catholic Church.

Since our Catholic children are going to take a lot of heat if they stand for authentic marriage, let's take a closer look at the issue of gay "marriage," why it is not ontologically possible, and why acknowledgment of this truth is not simply a "Catholic thing"....

Chapter Five
The Gay "Marriage" Juggernaut

When I first became a parent 25 years ago, I could never have imagined that one day I'd be raising children in a culture where gay "marriage" was put on par, legally or otherwise, with natural marriage. And yet now all of our children have been put into a situation where they will have to make sense of what is around them and will face the questions and accusations of their peers and others, most of whom have no grounding in the truth and meaning of human sexuality and marriage.

Here are the most common questions your children will be asked, followed by my answers:

"Why are you against gay marriage?"

It's not that I am against gay "marriage" per se, it's that gay "marriage" is an ontological impossibility. It's like asking why I am against square circles. Marriage has an essence, a meaning. It has always been a certain *kind* of union of persons, specifically a *conjugal* union rooted in biology itself; it is complementary and heterosexual by its very nature. The particulars of marriage contracts have varied over time and cultures, but the essence of male/female has not. Brides have always presupposed grooms.

The fact that marriage is what we might call a "universal" throughout human history indicates something huge, namely that we recognize this one particular type of personal relationship (male/female sexual union) as unique among all others. The reason should be obvious: It creates more humans. That children result from the union of man and woman (now father and mother) is the foundational reason that human societies have had a vested interest in protecting, elevating, and/or providing benefits for this type of union.

Without this sexual complementarity, and without the ability to have an actual union of bodies, there can be no marriage. With bodies of the same sex, the marital act physically cannot be completed; consummation is not possible. A bride implies a groom in the same way that a lock implies a key. Two locks make no sense together. Two keys make no sense together. The union of husband and wife, like the integration of lock and key, is a relationship different from any other.

"But what about heterosexual couples who are infertile? They are allowed to marry even though they can't procreate!"

The completed sexual union of male and female is always *ordered toward* procreation, even if the couple does not actually conceive a child. Age, illness, or a medical disorder of the reproductive system may render specific unions infertile, but those things do not change the *nature* of the sex act itself, which is *by its nature* generative. The conjugal union itself, and not the fruit of that union, is the seal of the marriage. Producing children is not the basis of a valid marriage, the conjugal union is. Whether or not children are conceived is beyond human control, and it's not the conception of children that makes a marriage — it's the total, one-flesh union of husband and wife, which is *by its nature* life-giving.

And as we've all known infertile couples who've eventually conceived years or even decades after their weddings, we can never say with certainty who will or will not be childless. God and nature have ways of surprising us. However, we can say with complete certainty that two men will never conceive a child from their sexual acts, nor will two women. **The sexual "union" of two men or two women is always barren, as nature and right order would have it**. That's not "unfair" any more than it's unfair that the heart pumps blood or that I have hazel eyes. That's simply the way it's supposed to be.

"What about men and women who are handicapped and not able to consummate? Are you saying that they cannot be married?"

This is a very delicate subject to discuss precisely *because* we have forgotten that marriage is a conjugal union. If there is no possibility of becoming "one flesh," not even one time, then the essence of marriage is missing. A relationship between two people without the ability to achieve sexual intercourse is called a friendship. That sounds cold to the modern ear, since we want everyone to feel good and "be happy," but feeling good at the expense of what is true can never satisfy, not ultimately. For marriage, one must be capable of performing the *marital act* (aptly named), at least one time.

Impotence or the inability to consummate is an impediment to the Sacrament of Matrimony for sure, but even the secular state will annul a civil marriage on the basis of non-consummation, which speaks to how universally and inherently humans understand the conjugal nature of marriage, whether civil or religious.

Now, with today's medical technology, thank God, there are many ways to treat or cure impotence and allow for marital relations. That is an incredible blessing.

"So you think marriage is all about sex! Can't you see it's about love?"

No, marriage is not "all about sex," of course, but sex is an intrinsic part of marriage. As mentioned above, a close and intimate relationship without sex is called a *friendship*, and neither church nor state would have reason to officially validate, elevate, or assign a special status to a friendship, as wonderful, important, and intimate as friendship is.

Also, while romantic feelings (what the culture calls "love") are ideal and desired between spouses, they've never been a prerequisite for valid marriage. To say they're required would be to deny that many of our own relatives and ancestors were actually married! My paternal grandparents, for example, did not know each other well when they became husband and wife. Yet they were married for over fifty years, raised five children while living in various war zones, immigrated to America, and have oodles of progeny. A particular feeling or emotion at the time of their wedding was not what made their marriage real.

Heck, if you ask Golde and Tevye (you all are huge *Fiddler on the Roof* fans like me, right?), they'd say their arranged-but-*consensual* marriage turned out just fine, even though they met on their wedding day. Yes, they are fictional characters, but they are representative of millions of valid marriages in the history of mankind. And we should note that their understanding of their love is closer to what <u>authentic love</u> actually is: a <u>choice. A choice to serve and will the highest good of the other, regardless of when or whether feelings of romance are present.</u>

"But the state says that gay people can marry, so that means they can!"

There are many things the state has said that are legal fictions, i.e., that are not true or based in reality. For example, governments have declared at various times by law that certain human beings are less human than others (slaves, Jews, the unborn), or that women are men and men are women (transgender laws). None of those laws can change reality. The law is not magic, and it cannot make some humans less human, it cannot make men turn into women, and it cannot make marriage between two men (or two women) possible.

The state can manipulate words, but it cannot change essences. The manipulation of words can certainly wreak havoc, however, and we should be very wary when any political agenda bursts forth in a frenzy, seeking to sever a culturally primal word (human, man, woman, marriage) from anything it has meant before.

Basically, when someone says to me, "Look, if the state says two men are married, then they're married!" this is what I hear:

> "Look, if the state says that cats can be dogs, then cats can be dogs!"

> "Look, if the state says that a woman can be a man, then women can be men!"

> "Look, if the state says that Jews are not human, then Jews aren't human!"

> "Look, if the state says that black people can be the property of others, then they can be!"

> "Look, if the state says that the unborn are not human beings, then they aren't!"

(Four out of five of those "truths" have happened, by the way.)

I teach my children not to lie. I will not go along with a lie. I will not teach my children to go along with a lie.

Marriage is pre-political; no state invented it, nor can any state redefine it. To illustrate how deeply this goes, consider the etymology (word origin) of the words "marry" and "matrimony" — they are derived from the word for *mother*, because marriage makes mothers! So, the meaning of the word "marriage" itself *excludes the very concept of a homosexual "marriage."* The very term "gay marriage" is self-refuting and self-negating.

Of course, the government can assign specific public benefits and provide services to whomever it wishes (that's within its legitimate authority), but what it cannot do is redefine an institution that is based in nature itself.

"How does gay marriage affect you, anyway?"

Contrary to conventional wisdom and the beliefs of many who pose this question, the consequences for marriage, children, society, and religious liberty are so numerous and far-reaching that this could easily turn into a multi-page answer. To spare you that, I have set up a link that will enumerate all the ways we are being affected and explaining how this will only get worse:

> http://littlecatholicbubble.blogspot.com/p/how-does-gay-marriage-affect-you-anyway.html

I will be adding to this webpage every time we and society are again affected. Sadly, the list promises to be quite lengthy.

"You should be concerned about all the ways that heterosexuals have weakened marriage!"

I am incredibly concerned about that! Divorce (especially the pernicious "no-fault" divorce), adultery, polygamy, polyamory, pre-marital sex, hook-ups, contraception, abortion, etc. All of that has gravely harmed the institution of marriage and, as always, children. But just because we've severely damaged marriage, that's no argument for demolishing it completely, right? The proper response to the sad state of marriage today is to strengthen it, not un-define it into oblivion.

Besides, every heterosexual marriage that is weak, irregular, or even broken has at least the *potential* to be strengthened, regularized and restored. But with two men (or two women), there is no potential for marriage in the first place (see #1).

I'll finish with this: While people often proclaim that there is no difference between traditional marriage and gay "marriage" — because "love wins" and "love is love" and all that — they know that it's actually not true. In fact, the essential mark of marriage, its intrinsic nature, must be cast off or put aside under the new paradigm. I saw this illustrated starkly when I came across the UK legal guidelines, intended for the public's information, on "How to Annul a Marriage."[5] I skimmed through the easy-to-read list of all the usual impediments that would warrant a civil annulment, and then I got to **consummation**, i.e., sexual intercourse, the one-flesh union that seals the marriage bond. A legal marriage, it states, is "defective" or "voidable" if it was never consummated (yep, sounds right) — but then comes the elephant-in-the-room caveat, placed parenthetically: "**(doesn't apply for same sex couples)**"

Blink. Blink.

So, consummation is an assumed, inherent part of all marriage — except for gay "marriage." Why? Because a same-sex couple cannot consummate a marriage, not ever. Gay couples cannot achieve sexual union, they can only simulate it. The government knows this, and deep down we all know this. Even a young gay friend of mine, who was "married" to his boyfriend (then quickly divorced), agrees with me privately (it's not something he can say publicly) that same-sex "marriage" is, in his words, an "**imitation** of heterosexual marriage." And yet the pretense goes on.

If even the civil law has to specify two different sets of rules for what we are told is "the same thing," then those two things are not actually "the same," are they?

This is the kind of reasoning our children must understand and be able to articulate in order to stay firm in their faith and in chastity.

Now let's tackle what chastity looks like for a young man, before and after marriage....

Chapter Six
Chastity Before **and** After Marriage

Q uick disclaimer: The truth and beauty of human sexuality and the virtue of chastity, as presented by Pope Saint John Paul II in his earth-shattering teaching on the Theology of the Body (TOB), is far beyond the scope and purpose of this book, much less this chapter. As a parent and simply as a Christian, you really must become familiar with TOB. To that end, I have included resources in the Appendix.

In this chapter, I offer only a snapshot of what chastity before and after marriage looks like, so that the very basics will make sense to your son.

An astoundingly common mistake, and one that I made for years, is to think of "chastity" and "abstinence" as synonyms. They are not. Sexual abstinence means refraining from sex, whereas chastity is a lifelong virtue to which we are all called in every state of life, including the married life. If that sounds confusing, let's look at how the Church defines chastity and go from there:

Chastity means **the successful integration of sexuality within the person** and thus the inner unity of man in his bodily and spiritual being. Sexuality, in which man's belonging to the bodily and biological world is expressed, becomes personal and truly human when it is integrated into the relationship of one person to another, in the complete and life-long mutual gift of a man and a woman. [CCC 2337, emphasis mine]

In other words, to be chaste is to live with sexual integrity. Sex is a privilege of marriage. In order to maintain bodily and spiritual integrity, an unmarried person lives out chastity by refraining from sexual activity; i.e., no sexual intercourse, no oral sex, no heavy petting, no touching or stimulation of one's own or others' genitals.

The self-mastery required for pre-marital chastity is not always easy, but it's always worth it. Since the marital embrace is the complete gift of self to one's spouse, body and soul, chastity before marriage preserves the gift while also preparing the man to be a better husband. From Catholic writer and professor Mark Lowery:[6]

You cannot have a healthy marriage without chastity — that virtue by which we are in control of our sexual appetite rather than it being in control of us. And chastity is a tough virtue to develop. If it is not in full development before marriage, it is going to be very hard to develop after marriage. So, before marriage is the time to accomplish this very positive thing, the virtue of chastity.

This is a courageous thing to do, a positive thing to do. **Males need to see it as the ultimate manly thing to do, and they need to take the lead** in the couple's mutual accomplishment of moral toughness. [emphasis mine]

Arleen Spenceley, a staff writer at the *Tampa Bay Times*, sums it up beautifully:[7] "Abstinence just challenges us not to have sex. Chastity challenges us to live lives in which desire is subservient to reason, which equips us to love as Jesus does: selflessly."

If our sons know to prepare well for sports competitions, major exams, and future careers, but are not preparing well for marriage — or for the priesthood, which is a spiritual marriage — they have missed the key training, the one which will sanctify them and bless future generations.

After the solemn marriage vows have been exchanged in the presence of God and His Church, chastity includes sexual union and is lived out freely, totally, faithfully, and fruitfully. There is nothing held back, no part of husband and wife withheld from each other, body or soul, including the astounding gift of fertility — just as God designed it.

Because we in the western world have been so thoroughly indoctrinated with the idea that contraception even for married couples is the "responsible" thing, and because even Catholic kids might shrug off contraceptive use as "no big deal," we must reorient our thinking and theirs. Our sons will naturally understand why adultery, porn, and spousal rape offend against chastity in marriage, but they may not fully understand why contraception does as well, so that's where my focus will be. Remember the principle we talked about earlier, that things must make sense to your child if you expect him to stand strong against the errors of the day.

Your children possess reason, and they can see that every created thing has a specific *nature* and *design*. When a thing is used according to its nature and design, it's being used correctly and will yield the very best of results. It's when we misuse a thing, or derail its design, that we get into trouble. This is common sense, and even a small child can understand it. (Ask your small child if a pen makes a good toaster!)

So, if we want to say that contraception is a positive good, then we also have to say that God's original design for sex and for our bodies was wrong, or at least was lacking something important. There's no way around it.

But let's think: When God was creating human beings, did He somehow "forget" that we needed contraception? Did He overlook or not understand that humans want to have sex without making children from that act? Did He accidentally connect pleasurable sexual union with procreation? Did the Creator mess up so badly that we needed to come in and add what He'd forgotten, or reconfigure the plan He botched?

Judging from the amount of times I've heard Christians say, "God gave us the brains to invent contraception," one might conclude that people *do* believe that condoms, diaphragms, spermicides, pills, patches, rings, sponges, caps, implants, injections, IUDs — and whatever other contraceptives I am forgetting — were a necessary improvement on God's first defective attempt.

However, when we talk about derailing our fertility, we are not talking about a disorder, defect, or disease of the body that needs treatment or fixing, such as when a failing heart needs medication, poor eyesight is corrected with lenses, a ruptured organ is repaired in surgery, or a missing limb is replaced by a prosthetic. We are talking about God's design for the body, which when working properly is called "health."

Of course it's silly to think that an all-knowing, all-powerful, all-good God made any mistake at all, much less a mistake involving the very mechanism He chose to bring new eternal human beings into existence. Obviously, God designed our bodies, our reproductive systems, and marriage exactly as He wanted. It is our "addition" of contraception (and our acceptance of surgical sterilization) that is the crucial mistake.

While it is true that various forms of contraception have been around since antiquity (as have abortion, adultery, fornication, masturbation and a host of other sins), Christians have always condemned it as gravely sinful. We've become so disconnected even from recent history that it's necessary to look back at just how widespread acceptance of contraception came to us, and how abortion came right on its heels, as the deadly fruit of a rotten tree.

On the secular front, eugenicist and atheist Margaret Sanger spearheaded the birth control movement with her 1921 founding of the American Birth Control League, now known as Planned Parenthood. Although Sanger herself did not champion abortion, she labored for contraception under the slogan "No gods, No masters" — a clarion rejection of Christianity.

On the Christian front, the acceptance of contraception began with the Anglican Church in 1930, when it cracked the door to allow contraception *only* for married couples, and *only* in serious situations — the "hard cases." By the following year, an association of Protestant denominations, the Federal Council of Churches, approved married couples' "careful and restrained use" of contraceptives.

It's important to note that at the time the birth control movement began, secular and religious sentiment had largely been in harmony regarding the evils of contraception (as happens with Natural Law issues), and condemnatory responses came from both camps.

The secular *Washington Post* editorial board wrote the following in a March 22, 1931 editorial, after the Federal Council of Churches endorsed the Anglican's 1930 Lambeth Conference condoning limited artificial birth control use:

> It is impossible to reconcile the doctrine of the divine institution of marriage with any modernistic plan for the mechanical regulation of or suppression of human life. The Church must either reject the plain teachings of the Bible or reject schemes for the "scientific" production of human souls.
>
> Carried to its logical conclusion, the committee's report, if carried into effect, would sound the death knell of marriage as a holy institution by establishing degrading practices which would encourage indiscriminate immorality. The suggestion that the use of legalized contraceptives would be "careful and restrained" is preposterous.

And Fr. Fulton Sheen, not yet a bishop, weighed in with his own prophetic assessment:

> Since a week ago last Saturday we can no longer expect them to defend the law of God. These sects will work out the very logic of their ways and in fifty or one hundred years there will be only the Church and paganism. We will be left to fight the battle alone — and we will.[8]

Many Protestant denominations were outraged by the Federal Council of Church's deviation from Christian moral teaching and put out statements of denouncement. However, within a few years, they all caved. Today, contraception as a positive good and a responsible choice is taught by all major Protestant denominations, with nary a reflection. Most Americans don't remember it being any other way.

By the 1960s, the hormonal birth control pill was all the rage, and it was touted as a boon and blessing to women, marriage, and family. Everything was going to be better now, the people were told. Even the Vatican's birth control commission, set up to study the question of contraceptive use and population issues, came out with a recommendation that artificial birth control should be allowed. But in 1968, Pope Paul VI rejected that recommendation and instead reiterated the unbroken teaching of the Church in his landmark encyclical, *Humanae Vitae.*[9]

Upon its release, the pope's document was met with disbelief, dismay, fury, mass disobedience, and widespread dissent, even on the part of countless clergy and, shamefully, bishops. Yet the encyclical's prophesies have all been borne out, including the following, which we see all around us today:

> [Contraceptive use will] open wide the way for marital infidelity and a general lowering of moral standards. Not much experience is needed to be fully aware of human weakness and to understand that human beings—and especially the young, who are so exposed to temptation—need incentives to keep the moral law, and it is an evil thing to make it easy for them to break that law. Another effect that gives cause for alarm is that a man who grows accustomed to the use of contraceptive methods may forget the reverence due to a woman, and, disregarding her physical and emotional equilibrium, reduce her to being a mere instrument for the satisfaction of his own desires, no longer considering her as his partner whom he should surround with care and affection.
> [#17]

The love in these words, the care of Holy Mother Church for the bodies and souls of her children, is so evident here!

Yet, this love was rebuffed along with the truth, and the rebellion raged in earnest.

As the law of natural consequences would have it, the acceptance of contraception swiftly led to the acceptance of abortion.

For example, Planned Parenthood went from peddling contraception to peddling abortion, and today it is the largest provider of abortion in our nation. The progression from contraception to abortion was natural and easy.

Similarly, many of the Protestant denominations that accepted contraception are now fully on board with abortion today. The Episcopal Church (the American branch of the Anglican Church) now officially and proudly supports abortion rights, as do many other mainline Protestant denominations. For much of Protestant Christianity, the progression from contraception to abortion has been natural (if not always easy).

Now let's look at how abortion came to us legally.

Roe vs. Wade was the 1973 Supreme Court decision that legalized abortion nationwide. A "right to privacy" legal argument was used as the basis for that tragic decision. However, most Americans are unaware that the "right to privacy" (words not found in the Constitution) did not originate with *Roe vs. Wade*, but with *Griswold vs. Connecticut* in 1965, and *Eisenstadt vs. Baird* in 1972. What were those cases? *Griswold* was the case that legalized the sale of contraception to married people, and *Eisenstadt* was the case that extended the same "right" to unmarried people. The "right to privacy" regarding contraception cleared the way for the "right to privacy" regarding abortion. The legal road from contraception to abortion was natural and easy.

Even the liberal justices on the Supreme Court of the United States (*Planned Parenthood vs. Casey*, 1992) understood clearly that contraception is a social contract that says, in essence, "We agree to have sex but we do not agree to have a baby." Because contraception fails so often, the contract needs a foolproof back-up, and that back-up is abortion. The Court, reaffirming legal abortion, put it this way:

> ...for two decades of economic and social developments, people have organized intimate relationships and made choices that define their views of themselves and their places in society, **in reliance on the availability of abortion in the event that contraception should fail**. The ability of women to participate equally in the economic and social life of the Nation has been facilitated by their ability to control their reproductive lives.[10] [emphasis mine]

It should make us sit up and take notice when the pro-abortion members of the Supreme Court *and* the Catholic Church see the same truth. Though on opposing sides of the abortion issue, both entities understand that contraception and abortion are symbiotically connected. How do they see so clearly what most Christians do not?

God's providence never fails us, of course, and each time sin and error ramps up, grace abounds even more: At the precise moment in history that the Pill stormed onto the scene, science was giving us ever-expanding knowledge of human fertility. Faithful Catholics who needed to postpone pregnancy went from using the largely unreliable calendar method ("rhythm method"), to the highly scientific and accurate methods of Natural Family Planning (NFP).

NFP and fertility awareness, which is permitted and promoted by the Church, is essentially information about how our bodies and our fertility work. This scientific information can be used not only to postpone a pregnancy, but also to achieve a pregnancy, help overcome infertility, and even assist women and girls suffering from menstrual disorders. NFP always respects and works *with* God's design, and, unlike contraception, it does not in any way change the nature of the marital act. It is completely compatible with the virtue of chastity.

Like TOB, NFP is a huge topic with many facets, and therefore is beyond the scope of this book. However, I've included resources in the Appendix, including a link explaining why using NFP to avoid pregnancy is most definitely *not* just another form of contraception.

By the way, all of the teenagers in the Miller house, both boys and girls, are presented with a solid overview of the science of NFP so that they understand long before marriage how incredibly ordered are our bodies. They know that we are "fearfully and wonderfully made" by the Lord, and that the gift and blessing of fertility is to be revered, not reviled.

Another common enemy of chastity has gained widespread cultural approval, and it's one of the biggest snares your boys will face....

Chapter Seven
Straight Talk About Masturbation

Never in my life did I envision writing an entire book chapter on masturbation, and I'm guessing it's not a topic that most of you would generally choose to read about. As I sat down to write this, I told the folks on my Facebook page about the subject matter, and the one-liners and double entendres that came forth (nothing vulgar, just some levity) were pretty amusing.

Indeed, the subject of masturbation is the fodder for many clever jokes and puns, but what really struck me is that while most of the jokers were faithful Catholics, one of my more secular friends responded to the topic of masturbation with a simple "Ick." That kind of sums it up, doesn't it?

It's an icky subject, and despite the "enlightened" talk of "healthy" masturbation — even by some Christian leaders who should know better — masturbation is an inherently shameful activity, and we all know it.

If you doubt that, then consider: We do not hear people proudly and openly discussing their prowess and expertise with masturbation. They may admit that they do it, they may even talk about it, but no one aspires to be the best at it. No one talks of how he has perfected his masturbatory techniques, and no one brags about high frequency: "I am the most expert masturbator there is! I masturbate more than anyone I know, and I am incredibly proficient at it! I'm what you'd call the master of masturbation!" Um, ewww. This is no way to attract the ladies, and even the guys in the locker room will likely keep a safe distance from the dude touting his special "talent."

By contrast, millions of men boast of their sexual prowess with others, both quality and quantity. We see this all around us, every day. We grew up hearing the "players" in high school and college discussing and embellishing their sex lives with pride. Then we have movie and television stars, musicians, celebrities of social media, sports heroes, corporate tycoons, many of whom would be thrilled to be known for their sexual accomplishments and abilities and hopeful for the press to advance that image.

Now, when men crow openly about prolific sexcapades *with others*, their hearers may either stand in admiring awe or scowl with disapproval, but they will not instinctively, viscerally *cringe* as they would at a loud and proud masturbator. Let's face it: Sex with a partner is one thing (even if sinful), but having "sex" with oneself is quite another.

Again, let's think about our human nature and how we were made by God. Each male and each female has exactly *one half* of a reproductive system. In fact, the reproductive system is the only system of the human body that is completed in someone else! Picture a male or female body in isolation, and it does not make any sense without the body of the opposite sex to complete the picture. The truth that the sexual faculty was made for *other* and not *self* is not some complicated, esoteric

riddle to decipher. It is plain. Sexual complementarity is written right into the design of our very bodies.

Every system of the body has a design and a right order for
use. Here's a rough analogy to the eating faculties:

The glutton often has no shame eating copious amounts
from the banquet table. In fact, like the sexual conquistador,
he may celebrate and publicize his accomplishments and pro-
clivities. He is doing something that the body is naturally ordered to do, i.e., eat and drink, but he's taking that good thing
to excess for pleasure's sake, and forgetting its inherent meaning, i.e., nourishing the body.

But the bulimic, unlike the simple glutton, does his deed in
secret. He is ashamed to expose his habit to others and would
never brag about how often and expertly he abuses his own
body by making himself throw up. The healthy body is not
ordered toward self-induced vomiting. It's not how we are
made, it goes against our nature, and it's a misuse of a bodily
system. Just as with the masturbator, there is an intrinsic
shame in misusing one's digestive system by manipulating its
functions against the natural order. In fact, we literally call bu-
limia a *dis-order* for that reason.

I want to be very clear about something here, because the
secular world is quick to misunderstand or misuse the word
"shame." Shame can be felt inherently from within, and shame
can be imposed on us from without. If I were to find out that
my child was masturbating or bulimic, I would not think of
"shaming" that child. Those acts are inherently shameful and
need no more shaming from me. While I might indeed tell a
child "shame on you" for proudly and *unashamedly* hitting his
sister on the head with a frying pan (same goes for an older
adolescent who started using girls for his pleasure), I would

never "double shame" someone for an act, namely masturbation, that is already naturally embarrassing or shameful.

So, the reproductive organs and sexual faculties are by nature ordered toward the other. Because human beings are body *and* soul — integrated — the human person flourishes when his intellect and his will are in tune with the truth of his body. We can convince ourselves to ignore and act contrary to our very nature (we do this all the time, to our detriment, and it's called sin), but somewhere inside, we know the truth.

That is why even populations that have been taught and believed the complete "healthiness" of masturbation have, to their own surprise, found freedom and restoration in giving it up.

Consider that a few years ago on Reddit (the wildly popular social news and networking site that gets hundreds of millions of hits a month), the "NoFap" community was born. NoFap is essentially a support group for those who take up the challenge to stop masturbating (and give up porn, its natural companion).

The group has tens of thousands of members, and though it is quite specifically *not* religious or moralistic in nature, it's led to a kind of redemption. As you can read for yourself on the "Ultimate Benefits" thread,[11] the fruit of living free of masturbation has led these men to wholly unexpected gains, including but not limited to:

More confidence
More control over all aspects of life
Feeling more like a man
Not as annoyed at others
Feeling more respect from others

Better relationships with women

Better memory and clearer thoughts

Better social skills

More motivated and productive

Better marriages (for married men)

Feeling more positive

Loss of mental fog

Lifting of depression

Feeling "alive"

Clearer skin and deeper voice (I know! But these were reported by numerous men!)

It should not surprise any Catholic that there are benefits to not masturbating. We know that virtue is at the heart of living a full and truly human life. We know that having self-control and integrity of body and mind is the key to interior peace and joy, and that if our intellect does not control our will, we are not truly free. But to those in the secular world, or those who do not fully embrace their own Christian faith, they are surprised and utterly delighted to find that the world without masturbation is a brighter, freer, more beautiful place!

We Catholics understand that by living according to our nature, human beings, human relationships, and human societies flourish. Folks like the ones on NoFap may not understand that explicitly, but implicitly, they are living it — and reaping the benefits of increased sexual and relational health, without even knowing (yet) that it's a spiritual triumph as well.

A huge point I want to make about masturbation, and that you have to tell your sons, is that *not everyone is doing it!* We and our sons would not know this if we listened to the voices around us. The general sentiment of the culture can be summed up in the words of Dr. Joycelyn Elders, U.S. Surgeon General under President Bill Clinton, who said: "We know that more than seventy to eighty percent of women masturbate, and ninety percent of men masturbate, and the rest lie."[12]

Of course this is ridiculous, and it's simply an attempt to normalize self-indulgence. One question I love to ask my boys when they are young is: "Who is the strongest man in the world?" Once we get past the excited shouted responses of "God!" (no, I mean human man) and "Jesus!" (no, I mean mere mortal, created man) and "Superman!" (no, not pretend superheroes), I give them the real answer: "The strongest man in the world is the one with the most self-control!" This answer delights a boy's imagination as he sees the sheer manliness of self-mastery in all areas. If a man can be strong and disciplined enough to become a star athlete, a concert-level musician, or a top scholar, he can certainly be disciplined enough to leave his private parts alone.

The Church is clear about the gravity of the sin of masturbation:

> By masturbation is to be understood the deliberate stimulation of the genital organs in order to derive sexual pleasure. "Both the Magisterium of the Church, in the course of a constant tradition, and the moral sense of the faithful have been in no doubt and have firmly maintained that masturbation is an intrinsically and gravely disordered action." "The deliberate use of the sexual faculty, for whatever reason, outside of marriage is essentially contrary to its purpose." For here sexual pleasure is sought outside of "the sexual relationship which is demanded by the moral order and in which the total meaning of mutual self-giving and human procreation in the context of true love is achieved." [CCC 2352]

Yet, she also understands the conditions that afflict and weaken a person's resistance to the sin:

> To form an equitable judgment about the subjects' moral responsibility and to guide pastoral action, one must take into account the affective immaturity, force of acquired habit, conditions of anxiety or other psychological or social factors that lessen, if not even reduce to a minimum, moral culpability.

So, while we must recognize that masturbation is intrinsically immoral, we must remember that anxiety, habit, and immaturity can lessen culpability. But even with lessened culpability, the sad consequences remain: An immature teen with anxiety who habitually masturbates will not find maturity, confidence, and social/relational health until he leaves this particularly addictive sin behind.

An important note here about scrupulosity. If you believe your son suffers from scrupulosity — a fear of sin that puts him in a state of debilitating anxiety — drop everything and get him help. An overly-scrupulous conscience is a serious hindrance not only to spiritual growth but also to daily functioning. Scrupulosity is a torturous psychological condition that we understand now to be one type of Obsessive Compulsive Disorder (OCD). Scrupulosity affects people of all religions (and no religion), but a Catholic with this condition may obsess over blasphemous thoughts that invade his mind against his will; he may agonize about whether or not something he's done is sinful, even when other faithful Catholics and his priest have assured him that it's not; he may have a conscience so hyper-sensitive that he cannot find peace with God; and he may fall into deep despair when he does sin. To help your child or anyone suffering with the hell that is scrupulosity, please refer to the Appendix for resources and help.

Ultimately, we do our boys and young men no service by pretending that just a little bit of sexual sin now and then will not harm them, will not distort their view of themselves and women, and will not quickly become addictive in this age of ubiquitous porn. For those not in the habit of conversing frankly about sex with their children, masturbation can be a difficult subject to broach — but just think how much more difficult things would be if you don't tell him and he becomes a compulsive masturbator who cannot become free.

That is a fearful thought, isn't it? Let's talk more about the place of fear in parenting....

Chapter Eight
Fear Has a Place

Yes, fear has a place, and as a big proponent of "be not afraid," I don't mean that one should live in fear. Not at all! But a healthy fear of sin and hell is a good thing, especially in the nascent moral life. A proportionate, well-ordered fear of consequences can help keep our boys on the narrow path.

Before we are fully morally developed, don't we avoid certain acts out of a reasonable fear of natural consequences? We teach toddlers not to touch a hot stove for fear of getting burned. We teach non-swimmers not to jump into the deep end of the pool for fear of drowning. We teach teenagers not to speed for fear of getting a ticket or crashing the car.

If a boy sees no negative consequence for a given act, or if there is no explicated downside to a sin that feels good, then why avoid that act or sin? In fact, that is exactly what the world is telling your sons — there is no reason to hold back on their sexual urges, as long as the sex is "safe" (masturbation! condoms!) and "consensual" (get a "yes" from your partner and then anything goes!).

When one is a young, healthy male, acting on sexual urges can seem like a great idea. Many teens and young men do act impulsively, forgetting — or never having learned — that a thing as powerful as sex has to have limits, context, and meaning. Teaching your children about human sexuality is your parental obligation, as we've already discussed in Chapter One, and raising a young male with no fear of sexual consequences is a bit like giving your third grader the keys to your car. People are going to get hurt, and badly.

Now it's true that choosing to do the right thing simply out of fear (of unpleasant consequences, of punishment, of damnation) is the *lowest* level of moral development, but some souls, including a good percentage of hormonal adolescents, need to start there. I'm going to assume that those reading this book are also filling in the other 95% of the story for their sons: the truth, meaning, and beauty of human sexuality, which is infinitely attractive to a seeking human soul. But in the fallen world, we need to hit that other 5%, too, as a healthy fear can be a good motivator, helping a young man in a weak moment or dark season of life.

I want to be very clear that when my husband and I apply the "fear tactic," it is accomplished very calmly, with no hysteria or drama on our part. It is quite matter-of-fact, simple, and to the point. Let me give you some examples of how I approach it.

When speaking to my sons about the dangers of porn, aside from talking about its inherent sins against women and human dignity (we don't objectify, commodify, and use people), I tell them that porn is as addictive as drugs, and that once a soul is drawn in and hooked, the devil has his foothold. I explain that pornography changes a man's very brain chemis-

try, and that extricating oneself from that addiction is a brutal
process, with some people not able to get out for years or decades, if ever.

I tell them how in the "olden days," porn used to be simple
photographs, two-dimensional nude women on a page, and it
was not so easy for boys and teens to get ahold of. Today,
porn is live, interactive, graphic, ever more perverse, depraved,
and violent. It's an infinite source of full-color filth and exploi-
tation, readily available at any and all moments to anyone with
internet access.

I explain that if they open the door to porn, they will crave
more and more of it, in ever-darker incarnations. I tell them
the truth that if they take that road, they will eventually be incapable of a healthy, normal, self-donative sexual relationship
with their wives one day, and that their wives, who will be real
human beings, will not be able to compete with the slick,
manufactured, slavish, airbrushed women on the screen. Their
wives will be crushed, neglected, rejected, and their marriages
will suffer and quite possibly break apart.

After this short discussion (repeated when necessary), porn
is reinforced as quite unmanly, quite beneath their own human
dignity. And to give them the bright side, and the hope of better things awaiting them, I remind them that according to a
secular study, devout, practicing Catholics have the best sex
lives![13]

Another example of how fear of consequences can motivate: I tell my sons that sleeping with a girl before marriage
could result in calamities that they have never considered.
Now keep in mind that my boys are profoundly pro-life, and
abortion is abhorrent to them. So they are shaken to their core
when I say, "Remember, Son, if you get a girl pregnant, there is

every possibility that she will abort your child and you will have no say in that decision. You have no legal rights at all, and you may not even find out about the pregnancy until after your child has been killed. You will have to live with that knowledge for the rest of your life." At this point, as is clear from their slacked jaws and wide eyes, they are sufficiently horrified.

I follow up with another common scenario that young men rarely consider: "If your girlfriend (or one-night stand) has your baby, and if she's not someone you end up marrying, you will still have her in your life forever, whether you like it or not. She will forever be the mother of your child, a child for whom you are responsible. You will have no say in how your child is raised (even if you get joint or partial custody, which may require considerable legal action and expense), nor will you have any control over the men or series of men and influences that will come into your child's life. There is no end to the complications that could come to all parties, especially to that innocent child who deserved a married mother and father."

And, although this may not be as convincing to an immature, developing teen (the frontal lobes of the brain are not even fully developed until 25), I explain that by having sex with someone out of wedlock, he could destroy a girl's trust and innocence, and break her heart into a thousand pieces. Would he be able to explain that to God?

On top of it all, I remind them that sexual sins, if committed with full knowledge of their seriousness and full consent of the will, can lead to eternal damnation. This is not a mere scare tactic, this is a truth of our Faith. It is unfair and unwise to shield our boys from the fact that the devil wants nothing more than to destroy innocence, poison marriages, and break apart families, all in an attempt to drag souls to hell. It's ridiculously easy for an un-warned, unguarded young man to be ensnared by sins of the flesh.

Before anyone freaks out (because frankly, I'm freaking myself out a bit by seeing the ugly truth of things laid out here in one small space), please know that Dean and I don't necessarily sit down and go over all of these points systematically in formal, austere meetings. It usually looks more like this:

We see porn discussed on TV, or we discuss pop culture, or we see a fast food commercial that is practically soft-core porn, or I see my sons on YouTube watching something innocuous (but am reminded of the garbage that is out there) and I might say, "Just remember, porn will rewire your brain and destroy your future marriage and your life, so don't even start down that road!"

I might get the annoyed "I know, Mom" in response, but often these little shout-outs open up longer conversations and we talk for a while. We understand each other and they really get it, because we've woven these discussions into our everyday lives previously (late-night discussions with teens are just the best, by the way!). The boys love God, they love their Faith, they love their family — including the little brothers who emulate and imitate them — and they don't want to be caught up in the sickness and sin they see all around them.

None of these interactions — long and involved, or short and off-the-cuff — is ever done tentatively or nervously. I speak with confidence and so should you. I am the parent. This is my job. Truth-telling and formation is my duty. I am sure of these truths, and I will not be deterred nor will I back down from my responsibilities and obligations before God.

Instilling a healthy fear of consequences can be a practical tool in your parenting toolbox. "Do not be afraid" to use it!

Now, lest you think we are a cranky, gloomy, fear-based family, and lest you believe us to be severe, mean, and puritanical, read on....

Chapter Nine
Navigating Pop Culture

This chapter is a tricky one. Some of the best and holiest Catholics I know, some of my dearest friends whom I admire greatly, will disagree with the Miller approach to pop culture that I am about to lay out here.

So I offer this heartfelt caveat: Take all I say in this chapter with the understanding that *this approach works for us, but it may not be right for your family.* Each topic I will discuss is for your own family discernment. If you vehemently oppose our approach, I will not be offended, but instead I will affirm you in your own approach. God has entrusted you as the parents of your children and you know them best. Parents are rightfully the primary educators of their own children, and these parenting decisions are matters of your prudential judgment.

For the Miller Family, as imperfect as we are, here's how we do it.

Jesus told us that we Christians are to be "in the world, not of it," and we take that to heart. "The world," of course, includes a whole lot of popular culture, some of it edifying and uplifting, but much of it base and degrading. Dean and I don't generally shield our kids from pop culture, but we give them the tools to discern. We make sure that they know that our Catholic principles and the moral universe are not shaped or defined by any specific era, society, fad, or fashion. The virtues are the same in any culture because they transcend every culture, and it is in teaching and forming our children in virtue that we inoculate them from the corrosive effects of the particular sphere they inhabit.

Our children know well that they are allowed to live "in" the world just as long as they realize they do not belong to it, they were not spawned by it, nor are their values and opinions formed by it. If I were to identify one rule that we have for our children in regard to pop culture, it would be this: "If your character starts to change, that's the end of [x, y, or z] for you!"

Let's break it down by subject.

Movies/Television

I'm not going to lie; we watch a lot of television, and my husband and boys go to see a lot of movies. I know, it's probably not ideal, but that is where we are at the moment. Who am I kidding, that's where we've been for decades!

But even with a steady stream of popular shows and films around us, our boys have remained strong Catholics, and chaste. So, how do we navigate TV and movies?

With regard to sex, this is our general rule: No overt sexuality exposure during the latency period. We shield and shelter our little ones. When folks say that parents should not shelter their children from the "real world," I say, "Of course we should. That's pretty much our job — to shelter them and protect their innocence."

We rarely watch the network channels anymore (thank you, Netflix), so we don't see many of the offensive commercials that could make adults blush. The little ones watch cartoons and kids' shows — until and unless those kids' shows start to showcase and promote gay "marriage," transgenderism, and the like, at which point those shows are off-limits in our home.

As far as movies, we don't follow a strict "no PG-13 movies until the child is 13; no R-rated movies until 17" rule. I fully respect and support those parents who do, but we take the movies on a case-by-case basis. Violence is not usually an issue in our decisions, as the context of most movie battles (good vs. evil) is okay with us. So far, we have not seen our boys become desensitized to violence, and except for the very occasional (and normal) brotherly brawl, they have never physically fought with anyone.

This is not to say that we allow the all the littles to see the violent stuff as a rule; even tonight, as I write this, my husband took our 16- and 11-year-old boys to a PG-13 action movie and left the 9- and 6-year-olds behind. We watched a cooking show at home while they were gone.

Just as each television show and movie is different, each child is different. As each show is evaluated, we discern for each child as well. For example, our family tradition is for the older members of the family to watch *The Passion of the Christ* on the night of Good Friday. As you know, this R-rated movie contains graphic violence that even my own mother cannot bear to watch. One of the little boys asked us for years if he could watch with us. When he was nine years old and younger, we said no, no, no. By age ten, we let him watch all but the scourging scene (although he became tired and didn't finish the movie). Finally, at age 11, he was allowed to watch it all. He suffered no ill effects and emerged with a deeper love and appreciation for Our Lord.

With the older teens, we generally trust their judgment when they go to movies with their friends, as they have proven themselves trustworthy in this area. They usually watch whatever Star Wars, true war story, action, disaster, or superhero movie is out. The adults and older teens in our family do enjoy movies like *Zoolander* and *Meet the Parents* (though we skip scenes when necessary), and I will admit to a summer-long binge-watching of all the old *Seinfeld* seasons with my then-17-year-old son (minus a few sexually explicit episodes that I nixed). We like to bond this way in the summer evenings — our latest binge being the *Survivor* seasons, by the way. This goes back to Chapter Two and the idea that it's okay to be your child's parent and his friend. I love kicking back, watching, and discussing my favorite shows and movies with my friends, including my sons.

Books

When our kids are little, we try to stick with the children's classics, history and historical fiction, Catholic stories, secular biographies, saint biographies, and other non-fiction, or innocuous entertainment including the popular series out there (everything from the *Magic Tree House* series to *Percy Jackson*, and more). We exclude children's books that preach political correctness or push gender identity theory, feminist ideology and the like. Most Judy Blume books are a no-go for my kids, but the *Harry Potter* books (which are controversial among some Catholic parents) are huge favorites in the Miller house, and we own them all.

For the teens, we don't monitor their books that closely, and we trust their judgment until their character changes or they give us a reason not to trust — something that hasn't happened yet. Yes, they like popular books, but they are also thoroughly immersed in the classics at their middle and high schools, trained to recognize the true, the good, and the beautiful in myriad timeless works. This Great Books education not only keeps them from seeking out literary junk, it also elevates their personal sense of virtue, character, and honor.

Music

Our younger boys don't have access to their own private iPods or CD players, etc., so they are mostly stuck listening to whatever we have on at home or in the car. By now you've guessed that we don't keep close tabs on what the older kids listen to, but we are happy that they dislike the most vulgar offerings out there. Dean and I tend to listen to country, the Eagles, most '80s music, and popular musicals, and the kids seem to share our tastes. We, parents and children, have enjoyed singing our lungs out to the likes of REO Speedwagon, Journey, and Billy Joel while on long trips or even at a concert attended together.

While we clearly don't limit the kids to "church music" or classical offerings, we also make it very clear how today's coarse, explicit, and degrading popular songs can corrupt a soul (or a generation), and that they must avoid it. They get it. Again, I am not sure how this all works, and it might not work for your family, but they get it.

Computers/Internet/Phones

We have no brilliant plan here. As far as computers, no child has his own computer until he leaves for college. There are two computers in the house for everyone's use. One is in the master bedroom, one is in the living room. Probably due to laziness (I'm keeping it real with you), we have yet to install anti-porn filters on the computers, so I cannot weigh in on their effectiveness.

Our children earn phones on an individual basis, but none of them have had phones before middle school, and most not until high school. The first three children had flip-phones only, and got smart phones either during college or after their engagement/marriage. Only one child so far has had a smart phone in high school, and even then not until he was in the upper grades.

All the minors living in our home know that any correspondence, whether by computer, email, text, or whatever, is subject to parental reading and review at any time. We are not zealously checking, but they are all aware that there is no "privacy" in our home when a child's safety, body or soul, is involved. Everything is open to inspection.

Video Games

Personally, I despise the male culture of video games. I am a hypocrite in some ways, however, as I love to play my own pet games on my phone (Ruzzle!). But there is something about seeing boys, teens, and young men playing on that stupid machine for hours and hours that makes me want to explode into irrational fits of anger (and I may or may not have done so once or twice…ish…). Of course it's not the boys' fault; my

husband and I are the parents after all, and aside from imposing some long hiatuses, we have not permanently pulled the
plug.

My advice is standard: Limit your sons' playing time, or
better yet, never get a video gaming system to begin with. Read
Richard Louv's *Last Child in the Woods* for some motivation and
courage if you need it.

There is something I want to mention that you might not
have heard before, though. Video games can be a way to let
off steam and work off tension, a good avenue of distraction
for those boys who are otherwise hard-working. Specifically
for our chaste young men, it's better that they have a video
game with which to wind down and de-stress rather than internet porn.

Before his recent marriage, my oldest son lived alone in a
small apartment in a tiny town 2,000 miles from his family. As
a medical student, he would study long hours, eat in solitude,
and often find himself quite lonely. He has told me that his
video gaming (usually played live with his younger brothers
across the country) was an excellent way to keep the temptation for sexual impurity and porn usage at bay. I think it's a
point worth considering, even as we make sure to warn against
gaming addiction.

Schools

When it comes to schools, we have done it all. Private secular
schooling, private Catholic schooling, homeschooling, public
charter schooling, regular public schooling, community college, state universities, etc.

In the early years of our decision-making, I remember being so relieved that "this is it!" and that there would never be a change in our schooling plan. And then God laughed and changed the plan — again and again and again. We have gotten to the point where we never say never about what type of school our children will attend. Each child is different, each school is different, and no school is perfect. We are grateful to have so many options today, and this is particularly true in Arizona, where choice in education is a tremendous blessing. A quarter-century into parenting now (with our youngest in kindergarten), we have learned to take things year by year, and sometimes semester by semester.

As far as the specifics of making school decisions, Dean and I are not closed to the feelings and input of our children, but we, and not the child, have the final say. I suppose I could write a book on the different schools and approaches we've taken over the years, but suffice to say that as long as your child is being catechized well, lives his faith, and is of good character, you are on the right track. If not, make a change.

Ideally, I would love to see every child receive a Great Books, classical, Catholic education, but that is not always possible. I've learned that, as long as a child is strong, secure, and joyful in his Catholic Faith, he can become the Light of Christ to others, leavening whatever schooling environment he inhabits. I've seen it happen first-hand, and not just with my own kids.

So, moms, don't beat yourself up if you cannot provide the "perfect" school environment for your children at all times. Do your best, watch your children's character, and make adjustments when necessary. Take every child and every school year as they come, and stay in Christ's peace.

Dating

My children did not do a lot of dating in high school, and in fact, only one child (our oldest daughter) had a steady boyfriend for a couple of years of chaste dating. The young man was a family friend and a practicing Catholic, and parents on both sides approved. My boys never really dated at all, aside from asking young women to homecoming or prom — mostly at my insistence, as I strongly believe that no gentleman should leave any young lady without a date to the big dance!

My feelings on teen dating are not set in stone, and we don't forbid it, but for some reason it's just never really been an issue. All three of my older children married young by today's standards, so when they did date, they dated with the purpose of finding a Catholic spouse and starting a family. We did not force or browbeat them into young marriages, and although we strongly encouraged them to marry practicing Catholics, there was no guillotine hanging over their heads; it's what they desired, thanks be to God.

Now, I do have a million and one opinions on the adult Catholic dating/marriage scene in general, but that's a whole other book!

Friends

One of the best things we ever did after my reversion and Dean's conversion was to find a community of like-minded, serious Catholic families, which provided our family, both parents and children, with a set of solid Catholic friends. For us, that community came by way of a tiny independent parent-run Catholic school that, although not a diocesan school, had the blessing of our bishop. The friendships that we and our children made there have lasted to this day, even as our oldest are adults.

Back in those early days, after we transitioned from living a largely secular life to a life of faith, it was a joy for us to see our children experiencing the Catholic culture as their norm. Families with five, seven, and even ten kids were just typical families to them. We worshiped God together at Mass, the saints were heavenly friends and role models, and a kid could go play at another kid's house without fear of conflicting values. I am forever grateful for our many years at not one, but two such Catholic schools, which felt like extended family.

Now that I'm an older and more seasoned mother, and now that my current littles have plenty of faithful older siblings as role models, a change in circumstance does not trouble my spirit. As I type this, not a single one of our children is attending Catholic school, and most of their classmates are not Catholic. As our family has grown big enough to be a society unto itself, and as we keep close to families from our old schools and current parishes, the younger children have enough support to sustain their Catholic beliefs, even as they enjoy their new friends. There are good kids everywhere, and character attracts character. So, know your child, know his friends, and make adjustments accordingly.

As you can see, our approach to navigating pop culture is not completely ordered, and we don't have a seamless plan. Let's face it, we are winging much of it as we go along! No doubt many of you have an even better plan for your family, one that has fewer gaps than ours. The most important thing is to pray often, stick to some basic principles that work ("when a child's character starts to change, we make a change"), and be at peace. God honors our efforts more than we realize.

When my kids become adults and move out of the house (as my fourth child did just days before I wrote this), I "let them go" as best I can from an emotional and control standpoint, trusting that the foundation we gave them is strong. All praise to God, the foundation has held steady for those who have already left the nest, and I pray every day that it will continue that way for the rest of the children coming up the line.

There is one kind of damage that popular culture (and political correctness) can cause our sons, however, which must be squarely faced and rejected. We will tackle that next....

Chapter Ten
Training Men out of Manhood

Many of the dangers our sons face are easy enough to spot. The red flags of early sexualization, the hook-up culture, pornography, and moral relativism make themselves clear enough.

But there is something more subtle that traps our boys. It's a steady drumbeat of dismissal, disdain, condescension, and disposability of men's unique gifts, contributions, and innate masculine nature. I call this "training men out of manhood," and it's insidious.

As an example, one feminist who blogs at *Plain Jane Activism* proudly identifies herself as a mother who "regularly annoys her 6-year-old son by staging peace talks with his action figures, and by grounding him whenever he attempts to rescue a princess."[14] My heart broke when I read this! This primal, vital, God-given instinct of a boy to be protector, provider, and hero is disparaged and made grounds for punishment by the first woman in his life.

While the attempt at some kind of social consciousness here may be well-meaning, this mother's approach is tragically misguided. Every boy and man wants to charge into battle as the knight in shining armor ready to defeat the evil villain for a noble and righteous cause. Good vs. evil is the thrilling, ultimate battle not only temporally but in the spiritual realm. The masculine heart is made for such things, and a small boy starts his training young.

And oh, the desire to rescue the damsel in distress should be cultivated! In this culture where so many women and children look in vain for good and protective men, why would we discourage our boys' intuitive desire to willingly sacrifice themselves for others, especially women and children who are in danger? If we dampen or, worse yet, punish this instinct in men and boys, we risk killing the part of them that gives them purpose and mission. And in fact, we deaden the very instinct that puts the "gentle" in "gentleman." Who wants a man unwilling to save the fair maiden but instead is quick to save his own hide? What is so terrible about "women and children first"? If chivalry is dead, it's largely because too many feminists, and even misguided Christians, willfully extinguished the protective instincts in their sons.

Our boys are floundering from too many cultural blows to their masculine identity. They need to be shown the path to manhood by other men, and when fathers are missing in their lives, as is too often the case today, we find many lost boys. Women, we can't take the place of men, but our boys do need us to understand and encourage the nature of a man.

As one of my favorite Catholic writers, Professor Anthony Esolen, says in one of his many brilliant essays on boyhood and manhood:[15]

> [A] woman who would lead boys must somehow see in them the fathers-to-be, the leaders of other men; and this

involves her in some difficulty. She wants to raise sons to be men who protect women, and who would not use their considerable advantage in strength and in tolerance for aggression and danger to put women at risk. But she cannot inspire boys with the noble calling of protector and provider while assuring them that they are no different from their sisters....

God Himself made male and female different. I had the privilege of sitting on the original working panel for Bishop Olmsted's *Into the Breach*. One of the presenters was Dr. Deborah Savage, a professor at St. Paul Seminary in Minnesota, who made a point that pretty much blew my mind and has stayed with me ever since: In the Book of Genesis, "[M]an's first contact with reality is of a horizon that otherwise contains only lower creatures, what we might call 'things' .... [W]oman comes into existence after man, [and] her first contact with reality is of a horizon that, from the beginning, includes man, that is, it includes persons .... [O]ther creatures and things around her appear only on the periphery of her gaze."[16]

This realization spurred and confirmed my understanding that we women are naturally relational and more oriented toward people, while men are more naturally oriented toward things. As Dr. Savage explains, men have a gifted capacity for understanding how to use the goods of creation to protect and provide for family and society. Neither disposition is better or worse, as each speaks to the respective genius of female and male. If we take away the particular "task" of man and his sense of mission — if he has no land to subdue, castles to build, or battles to win — we take away part of who he is, and he shrivels to something less than what a man was created to be. Women, and especially mothers: We must not diminish our boys' God-given sense of mission and identity!

I have no problem with my boys doing sword play or simulating duels or using fake guns. Cops and robbers, slaying dragons, or dreams of joining the military to "fight the bad guys" might be objectionable for some, but I don't discourage it.

One of the best conversations I have ever heard (and I promise, the only one on which I've ever seriously eavesdropped) was between my two oldest sons as they talked in their room late one night before bed. My older son was home from college, and the two young men were discussing self-sacrifice, dying heroically, and even the possibility of martyrdom. When my seventeen-year-old kept insisting that there is no more honorable or even glorious way for a man to die than to lay down his life for another (throwing himself in front of a bullet for a stranger, came one example), my maternal heart leapt with joy. Far from being anxious or worried about his desire, I felt so much peace interiorly, and gratitude to God for making great and noble the heart of my son.

I have never met a married woman who does not want her husband to take care of her and protect her. And I don't mean that she wants no voice, or she that wants to be a helpless little girl who can't do anything for herself, or that she wants to be dominated or controlled. The women I know are very strong, capable, and intelligent — nobody's fool. But when many of these same strong women hit rough patches in their marriages, they complain that their husbands are not "being the man." In fact, the exact words of many of these women are as follows: "I am tired of being the man. I need him to step up. I need to be taken care of sometimes. I want to feel like and be treated like a woman."

Think about that. None of these women are products of strict gender role-modeling from a 1950s detergent commercial. They are women raised in the '70s, '80s, and '90s, when "women's liberation" was already in full swing.

A while back I wrote a blog post in which I identified three types of men who support abortion. The first two — "the ignorant apathetic" and "the lech (or cad, or reprobate, etc.)" — are interesting to ponder, but it's the third category that is the most tragic in my mind, "the man trained out of manhood."

To illustrate this man, I took Barack Obama as an example. I don't mean to pick on him, but to me he is representative of so many other men raised and formed under similar circumstances. He is a man so lacking in the male protective instinct that he is fiercely committed to abortion at any stage and situation, *even to the point of voting to let a child die who survives abortion.*[17] How could this be? It makes sense if we consider his upbringing. As I said in the blog post:

> Obama was raised by a radical-leftist-secular-feminist-socialist mother. His father wanted nothing to do with little Barack, essentially abandoning him, and became simply a myth and a longing in young Barack's life and dreams. It's actually incredibly tragic to ponder, truly heartbreaking.
>
> So, this fatherless boy was not raised to know what it means to be a strong man who stays, protects, provides. He had no idea, and in fact the opposite was modeled to him by his absent, negligent father. Meantime, he had his strong, outspoken, and deeply committed feminist mother who taught him what a "man" should be, according to her radical template. Obama himself has described his mother, Stanley Ann

Dunham, as "the dominant figure in my formative years....
The values she taught me continue to be my touchstone
when it comes to how I go about the world of politics."[18]
He called her "a lonely witness for secular humanism."[19]

Not surprisingly, he grew up and married another strong
radical feminist, Michelle Robinson. Both these women
were and are the dominant forces in his life, and they no
doubt pounded it home to him that women have an absolute right to abortion. I'd be surprised if Barack Obama has
ever had a true friendship with a strong pro-life woman, or
even meaningful interaction with one. But the message he
received time and again, from all the women in his life — the
woman that raised and formed him, the woman that married him, and even the radical women he hung out with at
Columbia and later in politics — goes like this: "You *men*
have no right to tell us women what to do with our bodies.
We have a right to abortion on demand and without apolo-
gy. You are either with us on this most basic of freedoms,
or you are a misogynist brute oppressor."

What is a fatherless, lonely, ungrounded boy/man to do? I
can hardly blame men like this, because at least for a time,
they simply don't know any better. They defer to the wom-
en they love regarding "women's issues" and "women's
bodies" and "justice for women," because they really believe
it's not their place to speak. These men really believe that
this is how one "supports" women.

Much like the six-year-old son of the blogger I mentioned
at the top of this chapter, feeling shame about being a male is
what will drive our boys and men to snuff out or reject their
natural and rightly-ordered instincts to be protectors, providers, and leaders. These men, in increasing numbers, have perhaps never seen a truly honorable man up close and active in

their lives. Perhaps they have never known a male role model who keeps his commitments, protects and defends women and children, and is willing to lay down his own life for them before he'd consider harming them, body or soul.

The man trained out of manhood champions abortion, gay "marriage," "gender fluidity," no-fault divorce, and the radical feminism of today because he believes that's what he's supposed to do if he cares about women and humanity. He is left with an impoverished masculinity, and the whole world suffers for it.

Ladies, we have an important role to play: We must rejoice and affirm our boys when they want to do fake sword play with their brothers and friends. We must encourage the "hero" posturing and good guy vs. bad guy scenarios they dream up, even if the good guy wins by pretending to punch the bad guy in the nose, or by taking him out via dueling pistols in the Wild West. (One of my favorite home videos is an elaborate dueling scene between two of my then-little boys, filmed by their older brother, unbeknownst to me at the time. We all laugh about it and enjoy it to this day.)

When we allude to "boys will be boys" in my house, it doesn't mean anything like what today's feminists assume, i.e., license for boys to be oppressors, rapists, wife beaters. Nor does it mean what some fellow Christians say, that hey, of course boys will be masturbating, looking at porn, and having premarital sex, no big deal. In our house, it means that boys want to play the hero warrior, fight to protect the innocent, and defeat the bad guy. We could say more accurately that that's how boys will be men.

The precipitous decline in marriage and family life among our young men is a societal crisis, largely due to a lack of manly virtue. The aspiration for marriage, family, and fatherhood is strong in a virtuous young man and should be encouraged. As Pope Francis told the throngs of young people in Rio at World Youth Day 2013:

> Today, there are those who say that marriage is out of fashion; in a culture of relativism and the ephemeral, many preach the importance of "enjoying" the moment. They say that it is not worth making a life-long commitment, making a definitive decision, "forever," because we do not know what tomorrow will bring.
>
> I ask you, instead, to be **revolutionaries**, to swim against the tide; yes, I am asking you to **rebel against this culture** that sees everything as temporary and that ultimately believes that you are incapable of responsibility, that you are incapable of true love. I have confidence in you and I pray for you. Have the courage "to swim against the tide," Have the courage to be happy. [emphases mine]

The Holy Father wants our children to be rebels for marriage! Parents, encourage this "rebellious" desire if you see it in your sons!

Even if a man never actually marries and has children of his own, the desire itself is healthy and right. Again from Pope Francis, in his homily of June 26, 2013:

> When a man does not have this desire, something is missing in this man. Something is wrong. All of us, to exist, to become complete, in order to be mature, we need to feel the joy of fatherhood: even those of us who are celibate. Fatherhood is giving life to others, giving life, giving life...

And from Bishop Olmsted's *Into the Breach*:

Like masculinity itself, perhaps fatherhood has never been a widely-pondered topic among the philosophers because it has always been presumed, its meaning fairly obvious. This is no longer true. In his book, *Crossing the Threshold of Hope*, St. John Paul II writes of the attack on fatherhood in modern society: "This is truly the key for interpreting reality [...] **original sin, then, attempts to abolish fatherhood**." The great pontiff of the family points to our first parents' original act of disobedience, which cost them and us our original innocence and freedom from bodily death, and in original sin, we find a primordial rebellion against God's fatherhood, a desire to remove fatherhood itself. This is our enemy's underlying plan: to remove our reliance on God, the benevolent Father. To do this, **Satan's primary strategy is to damage and abolish human fatherhood, in the man and relationship where each of us first glimpses what God's fatherhood might be like.**

Also:

There are those in our culture today, however, who do not want us to see fatherlessness as unnatural or lamentable. **Do not be fooled by those voices wishing to erase all distinctions between mothers and fathers, ignoring the complementarity that is inherent in creation itself.** [all emphases mine]

We have a task ahead as we raise our sons to understand their own mission and identity *as men*. We must never concede even one inch to those who would have us train our men out of their very manhood.

Is this all just a pipe dream, though? Are there really any young men out there anymore who are strong and courageous enough to swim against the tide and embrace chastity and true masculinity? Oh, yes! Prepare to have your hope renewed as I introduce you to a few good men....

Chapter Eleven
Advice from Chaste Young Men

I asked several chaste young men, including my three oldest sons, for their answers to five questions:

1. What is the biggest challenge you face in this culture with regard to chastity?
2. Why do you remain chaste when others don't?
3. What do you say to those who would insist that you are lying about being chaste?
4. What advice do you have for (worried) parents who are trying to raise chaste boys?
5. What is your advice for boys/men trying to navigate this unchaste culture?

I wanted my sons to be totally honest and unguarded, and boy, were they — especially my oldest son. He pulled no punches, and I'm grateful for his honesty. His tone is firm and might seem too blunt for some of us mommies, but he is speaking the language that young men can hear (I even asked a few young men to read it first — they had no problem with it, even those who have struggled with these sins). If you consider boot camp in the military, there is a reason why the drill sergeants speak to the (mostly male) recruits that way. They hear tough talk from a man who's trying to whip them into shape, and they respond.

He is speaking to them as one who has "battled the beast up close," and he made it clear to me that he is directing these words to practicing Catholics, *not* to those young men who know nothing about the faith and the moral law.

Here is what my oldest son wrote as a 22-year-old single man (he is now 23 and married):

What is the biggest challenge you face in this culture with regard to chastity?

The biggest challenge is the constant temptation. The internet has unlimited amounts of pornography and erotica that is easily accessible. I live alone; there is no one to hold me accountable. I have to hold myself accountable. Despite actively avoiding this material on the internet, I will still sometimes find it unwittingly. This is the true challenge: to click that red x at the top of the screen before I lose my rationality. The other aspect of this is that in every modern medium, pre-marital sex and masturbation are treated as common everyday things that everyone is and should be doing. I once went to a urologist and he told me point blank that I should be masturbating — that it was normal! When I was younger, this used to make me feel very weird and different from my friends. It made me feel like an outcast. However, I no longer feel that way — I am not so easily swayed by peer pressure and have since realized that these people are slaves to their desires often in the same way animals are.

Why do you remain chaste when others don't?

Multiple reasons:

1. I have a true understanding for the purpose of sexual faculties. That it is to be both unitive and procreative, and that any misuse of this is a grave sin. Sex is not just about pleasure for pleasure's sake. It is giving the whole of yourself to another in sacrificial love. Any distortion of this act is inherently selfish and immoral.

2. I view masturbation as one of the most pathetic and harmful things a person can do to themselves, and as such I avoid it. To me it is childish, and just plain gross. Why would I want to have sex with my hand? We are not made for it, we are made for something much more beautiful. It follows that since I despise masturbation so, I would remain chaste.

3. I have a fear of Hell, and offending God. It is such a profound fear that I would never even consider masturbating or having pre-marital relations.

What do you say to those who would insist that you are lying about being chaste?

I probably wouldn't say anything. They can think what they want; it does not affect what is true. However, for the purpose of the question, I guess I would ask them why I would even lie about such a thing? If masturbation and sex are so normal and commonplace, why would I want to appear the outsider? Why, if 97% of men are [masturbating] daily, would I put myself in the 3% that don't? Why would I make myself look like a freak?

What advice do you have for (worried) parents who are trying to raise chaste boys?

From the start, have an open door policy with your boys. No question should ever be off limits. Do not shame them for wondering, and do not chastise them for being curious about the female form. When I was younger, about 12, I was on Amazon, and a photography book that had a naked woman on the cover caught my eye. I clicked on it and stared at the pictures until my mother caught me. I was ashamed, obviously, but she thought it more funny than anything. The point is, she did not shame me or punish me, she explained that I should not view such things and, more importantly, WHY I should not view them. Always give a reason, and if you don't know why, find out! You will earn their respect and trust, and they will always come to you first with questions.

Do not be afraid to teach basic female anatomy to your sons at around the time you have "the talk" with them. If you do not teach them about this stuff, they will inevitably take to the internet to find out for themselves and may be exposed to some very nasty stuff in the process. Teach them that the naked human body is not something to be feared or disrespected.

What is your advice for other boys/men trying to navigate this unchaste culture?

Stop touching it. Seriously, control yourselves. The act of masturbation requires many steps, all of which, at any point, you can stop. In the same way, the act of pre-marital sex requires conscious choices. You don't "accidentally" have sex. You are called to be strong men, not juvenile children hiding in their closets. If your computer leads you to sin, smash it. Rise up; you are not a slave to your passions. You are a man with free will. You have the power to choose. And remember that you have no legitimate excuse for your actions. We will always try to justify our sins, since we are human after all. But your justifications are as pathetic and harmful as the act you are about to inflict upon yourself. Be a strong, God-fearing, selfless man.

Next, my 18-year-old son gives his responses:

1. The biggest challenge I face in the culture is probably that everyone just accepts unchastity to be normal. Everywhere on TV or at school people present these sins as something that everyone does or something everyone should do. I've never been unchaste or sinned sexually, so it's not that hard for me to maintain that. It's not hard to continue not doing something. It's annoying that the culture today is so tolerant of such things and assumes that if everyone is doing it, it must be okay.

2. I remain chaste because I know it's a sin and understand why it's a sin. A lot of people probably have been told that it's wrong, but not why it's wrong. If it's not harming anyone, how could it be wrong? Telling someone it's wrong is not enough. It is important to understand why, in order to know that you shouldn't do it. That holds true for all sins.

3. If people think I'm lying about my chastity, it makes me disappointed that people think I can't have self control. Other than that, I'm not bothered by it because God knows that I'm chaste and that's all that matters anyway. People are allowed to be wrong.

4. For parents, I would say trust your kids. Give them the benefit of the doubt. If you have explained to them why these acts are sinful, it should be enough to keep them chaste. After

you teach them why it is a sin, it's really out of your hands whether or not they keep their morals. It's between them and God.

5. For other boys and men, stay strong in the face of society. Prove everyone else wrong. It will pay off in the end. Waiting until marriage to experience sexual pleasure is probably the best way to experience it. Don't ruin that. It's not how God made us.

And from my 15-year-old son (funny how the words are fewer the younger they get):

1. My biggest challenge is when I see an attractive person, I try not to think of lustful things. It's easy to think of lustful things, so I challenge myself not to.

2. I first find other things or hobbies to keep my mind occupied. Also, I would never want to say those sins to a priest in confession, so it helps keep me in check.

3. I would tell them that I'm not lying, but they can think whatever they want to think.

4. There is nothing you can do to stop your kids. But teach them right from wrong and hopefully they will make the right decision.

5. Try to find other things to occupy your mind. It is very easy to sin, so find something else to replace it.

I was also able to ask several other young men from around the country the same questions. Their answers are incredibly hopeful and, I believe, helpful. The following are some excerpts from their answers.

In response to the first question, **"What is the biggest challenge you face in this culture with regard to chastity?"**

From a 22-year-old engaged man:

When I was in college, I remember my roommates and I throwing a party at our house for Super Bowl XLIX. Keep in mind that the Super Bowl is the biggest television event in the US every year with most of the viewers being a male audience. During the halftime show, Katy Perry initially came out dressed in clothes that covered her body more than usual. This prompted one of my roommates to exclaim something along the lines of, "She's wearing too much clothing! I can't see any of her!"

Those two sentences really summed up our culture in a nutshell. Much to my roommate's delight, and to my dismay, Katy Perry didn't stay like that and she gradually took off much of her clothing as the show went on. This is what we are up against. We have a culture that expects women to act like sex objects while men can continue to indulge themselves in their lustful fantasies. What my roommate said was very symbolic of our age: down with chastity and up with lust.

From a 16-year-old star high school athlete:

The biggest challenge for me is the influence from my friends/students/teammates.

From a 22-year-old who is "loving chastity":

Advertisements. Most advertisements are porn. They don't sell a product, they sell sex (or sex is the product). Throw in movies and TV shows. All of these things are more often than not pornified. These things are all the propaganda of an unchaste culture.

From a 24-year-old engaged man:

Because I was open about believing — as the Church does — in abstinence before marriage, I was ridiculed by males and patronized by females. The feeling, thus promoted by society, that one is not a real man unless he is having a lot of sex and is very good at it, can be a huge challenge for a young man trying to maintain his virtue.

From a 23-year-old Catholic seminarian:

Temptations toward unchastity are literally everywhere! The most challenging thing is that, while there are certainly a lot of overt sexual themes on TV and in movies and advertising, the temptations and the things that lead to unchastity are usually much more covert.

The constant promotion of individuality, of moral relativism, and the necessary indulgence of every desire (carnal or otherwise) creates a culture in which anything goes and everything is acceptable.

From an 18-year-old Catholic seminarian:

By far the biggest obstacle to young men striving to be chaste is the omnipresence of suggestive material in everyday life. Many chastity speakers and writers emphasize the destructive nature of things such as TV commercials and magazine covers, but the impact of images on the minds of boys simply cannot be conveyed in a few words....For me in our current culture, normal activities like watching a football game or buying groceries become mentally excruciating and spiritually dangerous.

From a 15-year-old high school student:

Being a student at a public high school, many of my peers often ask if I want to view nudes of any of the various women on campus. The hardest thing to do is tell them no, not only because I am often tempted to view them, but also because of peer pressure, which can seem worse than the temptation of looking at the photos.

From a 22-year-old man:

For me, I have found the biggest challenge lies in how our culture tells women to behave. I have, on more than one occasion, had to call things off with a girlfriend because she felt that sex needed to be part of our relationship. The "everyone else is doing it" mentality has certainly been ingrained into men and women in our society and that can be challenging for men such as myself. I won't lie and say that calling things off was easy; in fact, I was engaged to one of these women, but a strong foundation and constant support from my family helped.

From a 24-year-old man:

The most difficult part is the influence of peers and culture being thrown in your face. The fact that you have to face it when you do anything. Even in your own home on the TV and computer. You have to become a hermit to avoid it and even that is difficult. To function in society you must be exposed to sexually explicit material. Because we have become accustomed to little things like mild jokes and what-not, we don't even know we are being weakened.

Excerpts from responses to the fourth question, **"What advice do you have for (worried) parents who are trying to raise chaste boys?"**

22-year-old engaged man:

When boys are educated in chastity, it needs done in a way of understanding about their bodies and it should be open enough for them to ask questions. If the education is too harsh, they may become ashamed of their bodies, even if there was nothing to be ashamed about in the first place. If the education is too lax, or worse there is no education, then the boys will learn from the culture. It is also important that it is not a one time "talk" and nothing else. The education needs to be continuous since boys progress through more body changes as they grow older. The communication line must be kept open so that they are comfortable to ask questions whenever they have them.

16-year-old star high school athlete:

Just raising your kids in a faith filled environment. And allow your kids to open up to the faith. Send them to youth conferences like Steubenville. This transformed my faith from something you have to do into something you want to do.

22-year-old who is "loving chastity":

Do not worry. Do not be afraid. Talk to your boys about sex and love, and do not shy away from it. I know many parents who decided not to talk to their children about sex until they are such and such an age, and even then it's a one time, vague conversation about "the birds and the bees." When this happens your children will learn more about sex from their friends at school and teachers in health classes than from you.

Sex is beautiful, love is amazing! I know you think sex is amazing and beautiful! Why do you shy away from telling your kids about it? Do not make the "sex talk" a one-time thing. Make it a continual conversation, starting when they are young.... Most importantly though, love your spouse. Wives kiss your husbands, husbands kiss your wives, in front of your kids. Let them see the affection you show each other. Show them how devoted you are to each other. Show them how you chastely live in marriage. This is an infinitely better lesson than using words.

23-year-old Catholic seminarian:

Don't try to hide the culture from them or them from the culture; when they inevitably go out into the world they won't be ready for it, first of all, and second their reaction will be like a broken spring: the tightness that once protected them will turn into the force of their demise. I hope that makes sense.

Set clear rules about technology use, acceptable behavior with women, but don't criminalize their sexuality.

So....culture of chastity, openness with your kids about their struggles, non-judgmentalism.

18-year-old Catholic seminarian:

If you as parents see or sense worldliness or an unchaste spirit in a peer or companion, ensure that your child parts ways with the young person. Do not be afraid of appearing harsh or unreasonable.... It took me 17 years to encounter chaste and Godly men for friends, but such blessings they have been to me that I would go back and wait to meet them anew.

22-year-old man:

My biggest word of advice would be to establish a strong sense of communication. I have always felt that I can come to my parents with any questions or problems I have had, and that has certainly helped. As I mentioned before, I had to call off an engagement with a woman I had been in a relationship with for many years, and this was because, among other things, an issue of chastity. The communication my parents offered to me helped me through this process more than I can ever say, and I can't thank them enough for it. I think with a strong line of communication, parents can convey a strong message of chastity that will permanently be instilled in their boys.

A young married man looking back on his single years:

I would tell parents to talk about chastity in age appropriate ways, starting as early as the age of reason and not shrinking from the subject, especially when they become awkward teenagers.

24-year-old man:

This one is very difficult. Obviously the first and most important thing is for parents to pray. I've seen many good parents have children become sex addicts and leave the faith. On a side note, most young people I've known have left the faith for sexual reasons. They slept with someone, decided not to go to confession and that was it. I think if parents lead a good example and don't obsessively enforce it, children naturally will follow them.

∼

There is so much more that these incredible — and utterly normal — young men have to say. Those of you with older boys might want to refer them to the webpage where I have posted all their advice for young men, which was too long to include here. I will leave you with a couple of their nuggets of wisdom specifically directed at your sons:

♦ Take the long and narrow road. Find good and encouraging friends, men and women, to keep your perspective clean. Do not waiver in the face of adversity, because if

you do, you will be less of the man that you were created to be, and to get back that which was lost is a rough
and rugged road. You will not die if you do not give in;
trust me.

♦ Above all, be courageous, and be such a man that other
men will look at you and say, "Christ abides in him; I
wish to possess this fire also."

To read the young men's complete answers (believe me, it's
worth it), go to:

http://littlecatholicbubble.blogspot.com/p/raising-chaste-
catholic-men-young-men.html

Despite our best efforts, however, sometimes things go
wrong....

Chapter Twelve
When Things Go Wrong

After all your blood, sweat, and tears, and after countless hours in supplication to God and His Mother for your children, it could be that your son will grow to adolescence and regularly commit sins against chastity despite your best efforts. Maybe that's already happened. Before you fall into guilt, self-reproach, anger, anxiety, depression, or despair, memorize these two hard and fast rules:

Rule #1: Do not freak out!
Rule #2: Refer to Rule #1.

Freaking out will accomplish absolutely nothing, and you want to stay away from anything that is non-productive.

Your job at this point is to remain steadfast in the truths of our Catholic Faith, while staying available and open to communication. Continue to show affection and love to your child, no matter what he has done. God does not love us with conditions, nor does He abandon us when we sin, and so we must follow His example of unconditional love for our own sinful children, who are still and always precious to us, made in the image and likeness of God. Remember, though, that loving and cherishing him does not in any way mean accepting, condoning, enabling, or encouraging his sins.

Most importantly, your job is to pray. A call to prayer may sound trite and useless when a beloved child seems happy with (or addicted to) his sin, but nothing could be further from the truth. It is in this situation that you, dear mother, are a modern-day St. Monica. She prayed many long years for her wayward adult son, Augustine, whose Achilles' heel was lust. He was unable or unwilling to fight the beast of unchastity for what must have seemed like an eternity for his poor mother. He lived with and used women, fathered a child out of wedlock, and still came to be one of the Church's greatest bishops and saints, a champion of chastity, and a Doctor of the Church. He credited his mother's prayers as key to bringing him from darkness to light. She was despairing of hope for her son, until a saintly bishop advised her that "the son of so many tears could not perish."

Far too many stories of conversion fill Christian history and even our own little spheres of life to despair of any soul, much less our own precious sons caught up in their sins. The story of sin and redemption is, in fact, the story of humanity itself. To save us from our wretched sins is the very reason Jesus Christ came in the Flesh and died on the Cross! Though we'd never consciously want to push it this far, our Faith teaches us that we each have until our last breath to repent and turn to God, and that the Lord will give us all the graces necessary to do so. We need only choose to cooperate with those graces.

For those of you who do not have a supportive spouse (or any spouse at all) by your side in this fight, remember that St. Monica was alone in her fight for her son as well. St. Augustine's father was a pagan until late in his life, when he finally accepted baptism and went to a holy death, thanks to the influence and example of his faithful wife.

Without the benefit of a healthy, happy marriage serving as an example to your children and creating a unified front for your sons, the task of raising chaste young men is certainly more difficult. But we know as Christians that the task is not impossible, it simply means you'll have to double-down on making the Faith seem reasonable and stable in a world gone mad.

Our Catholic Faith is the shelter in a storm, the one thing that will never change and that your son can always count on, even if his own family has been rocked with uncertainty, lack of stability, confusion, and pain. It is precisely for the lost, for the wounded, for the broken, that Christ came. "The healthy have no need of a physician," after all.

The Church, including her teachings on chastity, is balm for the wounded soul. She is the rock-solid foundation for the boy who feels like he's been placed on shifting sand as a fatherless male or a child of divorce. The attraction to the Church is potentially even bigger in your household than in others, because it's a golden lifeline of truth and hope offered to a young man who is at greater risk of sinking in cultural quicksand.

My husband Dean was raised in a secular Jewish household, witnessed decades of his parents' always-unhappy marriage, and was not schooled in the virtue of chastity (quite the opposite, in fact). If we speak of ideal conditions for understanding and embracing that particular virtue, the deck was stacked against Dean a mile high.

However, a small, still voice in all of us speaks of timeless truths and the dignity of our own humanity. We were made for more than pleasure-seeking and comfort, and somewhere inside, every boy and every man knows this.

Something in Dean held him back from being the cad that he easily could have been, and by the time we discovered the fullness of Catholicism together (after six years of marriage and three children), he was ready to embrace the virtues enthusiastically. And as evidence that we can never know the full depth, breadth, and beauty of God's plan, a full twenty years later Dean helped to lead his Jewish/agnostic/New Age divorced mother to Christ. Partly due to the example of her son and our family, Carol was baptized, confirmed, and received Jesus in the Eucharist in August of 2013. And after having lived the majority of her 67 years without God, she died a holy death with the sacraments of the Church just 15 months after her conversion.[20] God is good, and He is pleased to work with our wounds and weaknesses to bring about grace-filled miracles for His glory.

There are specific and practical things that can help you as a mother without a supportive spouse. Mike Phelan, the Director of Marriage and Respect Life Office for the Diocese of Phoenix, who has dedicated his life to addressing the crisis of manhood, has this advice to share:

> Remember that God has not abandoned you or your son, even if the husband/father has. Embrace the "work of trust in God" necessary and make time to become true and wise disciples of the Lord, and to heal where needed. You especially must not take shallow and harmful solace in dating

other men until they have experienced significant healing. You are called to radical trust, deep discipleship, holiness in the face of difficult odds.

Though you are a true, true hero for your stalwart presence with your children, you cannot be a father, and you should not embrace the silly cultural illusion that you can be. You must pray hard and look to ask healthy men who have time to be father figures for your children, especially your boys.

And to men reading this: it is time for a movement of healthy fathers and grandfathers at parishes to step into this breach and provide counsel, time, and a fatherly model to these abandoned and "at risk" boys. These boys and their mothers are the "widows and orphans" of our time, and God is calling us to step up.

It is imperative that you not despair for lack of a perfect situation (remember that discouragement is from the devil, never from Christ), but answer the call to personal holiness, wisdom, and knowledge; take every opportunity to make yourself an amateur expert on the teachings of human sexuality, on the vision of the Church, and on the design of God's creation. Be sure to enlist others around you for support.

And a word for those wayward or missing fathers, if any are reading this, from Bishop Olmsted's *Into the Breach*:

Catholic men also contribute far too regularly to this same scandal that devastates the heart of a child and makes too many women in our culture live as if they were widows! The ache of the fatherless child's heart cries out to Heaven: "He will not ignore the supplication of the fatherless, nor the widow when she pours out her story...and the Lord will not delay, neither will He be patient with them, till He crushes the loins of the unmerciful and repays vengeance on the na-

tions" (Sirach 35:14, 18). Why do the widows and the fatherless cry out? They have lost their protectors and providers!
There is an unnatural void of the one called upon by God
"to ensure the harmonious and united development of all
the members of the family." It is because of this loss, this
void caused by men's absence, that we have always naturally, traditionally, lamented fatherlessness.

... Men, your presence and mission in the family is irreplaceable! Step up and lovingly, patiently take up your God-given
role as protector, provider, and spiritual leader of your
home. A father's role as spiritual head of the family must
never be understood or undertaken as domination over others, but only as a loving leadership and a gentle guidance for
those in your care. Your fatherhood... in its hidden, humble
way, reflects imperfectly but surely the Fatherhood of God,
the Father to those whom the Lord has given us to father.

Here is the most important thing to take away from this
chapter:

Whether you are single, unsupported, or have the full support of a faithful Catholic husband, the good news is that, if a
child falls away from the Faith, you are not helpless in the battle for your sons' souls. You may not have considered that *you
can make your prayers more powerful than they are right now.* How?
Become a saint! That is not a platitude, it's the plain and simple truth — and it's something we don't hear enough. We hear
that we should pray for our children, but we forget that as we
ourselves become more holy, more abandoned to God's will,
more dead to self, more detached from this world and at-
tached to God, the closer we come to the heart of the Trinity.

The saints in union with God, both in Heaven and on
earth, have no barriers between themselves and Christ, and
their prayers are explosively powerful. Scripture tells us, "The

prayer of the righteous is powerful and effective" (Jas 5:16), so work toward righteousness! Become a saint! What is stopping you? What else matters? There is nothing else that we are ultimately called to do anyway, so get to it. And in the process, you will help to save the souls around you with an overflow of grace in your own soul. God wants not only the sanctity of your sons, after all, but of yourself. Make holiness your mission, and watch what happens to those around you. Miracles of grace follow saints wherever they go.

Which brings me to something I consider crucial and non-negotiable for all Catholic families whether intact or not: *Make the practice of your faith a joyful one.* Children who see their childhood religion as a source of misery, strife, anxiety, harsh judgments, dour faces, and/or humorlessness will surely turn away from it the first chance they get.

But if your child's experience of the Faith is affirming, loving, merciful, welcoming, and *joyful,* then he will associate his Catholicism with joy. And if he should still stray from the Faith? Well, when the world starts to let him down, disturb him, cast him into darkness, and even eat him alive — which it eventually will, given enough time — he has a firm foundation to come back to someday, and a soft place to land.

If, throughout our children's childhoods, we worry and fret and hand-wring for too long, we are not only failing to trust in an all-powerful, all-knowing, all-good God, but we are telegraphing to our children that we are afraid, or that the world is spinning out of control. As believers in Divine Providence we know that the world is in the hands of our loving Father, and He can be trusted. We do our part, and He does His. Relax and trust Him, and teach your children to do the same.

At every turn, especially when things with our children go wrong, we cling to **hope**, that theological virtue that is not simply "optimism" but rather a belief in the *certainty* of God's promises, and thus we remain in His **joy**.

Let's end our conversation with a few final thoughts....

Some Final Thoughts

We've come to the end of our conversation together, and although we have discussed many important things, we have left so much more unconsidered.

If I had you in front of me now, if you had gathered up your belongings to head home after our mom-to-mom talk at my kitchen table, I would grab you and put my hands on your shoulders, look you straight in the eye, and tell you the following, from my heart:

> "Talk to your sons. Keep the lines of communication open, always. Keep your sense of humor no matter what. Never compromise your Catholic Faith, but always live it out. Let your children be able to say of you, 'Her faith and her life were never separate.' Speak in terms of virtues and not 'values.' If you are married, keep your marriage strong. Be a witness for chastity and for marriage in a thirsting, hurting world that needs to see it. In doing so, you will be a beacon for many weary souls, including your own children.

"Read the Scriptures and partake of the sacraments often. The Eucharist is the source and summit of the Christian life because the Eucharist is Christ Himself, Body, Blood, Soul, and Divinity. Go to Mass and Adoration. Bask in His glory, be with Him, adore Him, consume Him — as He, in turn, consumes you. Go to Confession frequently and take your sons. The graces received there are real. The sanctifying grace of the sacraments is the very life of God, which will carry us to Heaven — and that has been the goal all along.

"Do not be afraid. Of anything. God is in control of, and is much bigger than, this world. He cares for you as tenderly and lovingly and personally as you care for your own child — except infinitely more. Pray to Him. Rest in Him. Be at peace. Then do your best and let it go."

Then, I would give you a hug and let you be on your way. You've got sons to raise.

And when night comes, and you look back over the day
and see how fragmentary everything has been,
and how much you planned that has gone undone,
and all the reasons you have to be embarrassed and ashamed:
just take everything exactly as it is,
put it in God's hands
and leave it with Him.

St. Teresa Benedicta of the Cross
(Edith Stein)

Appendix

For all the information below *plus* many more resources and links not included here, simply go to this address:
http://littlecatholicbubble.blogspot.com/p/raising-chaste-catholic-men-appendix-and.html
I will be updating and adding to that page periodically.

THEOLOGY OF THE BODY (TOB)
Theology of the Body for Beginners, Christopher West
Good News About Sex and Marriage, Christopher West
http://thetheologyofthebody.com

CONTRACEPTION
One of the best overviews I've read:
http://www.thepublicdiscourse.com/2016/08/17559/

NATURAL FAMILY PLANNING (NFP)
The basic science of it:
http://littlecatholicbubble.blogspot.com/2011/03/the-natural-
family-planning-post.html
Why it is not simply "Catholic contraception":
http://littlecatholicbubble.blogspot.com/2011/03/important-
follow-up-to-natural-family.html
From the US Bishops:
http://www.usccb.org/issues-and-action/marriage-and-
family/natural-family-planning/catholic-
teaching/upload/Chastity.pdf
How NFP works in real life:

The Sinner's Guide to Natural Family Planning, Simcha Fisher

NATURAL LAW

What We Can't Not Know, Professor J. Budziszewski
On the Meaning of Sex, Professor J. Budziszewski

GAY "MARRIAGE"

For many legal and social implications:
http://littlecatholicbubble.blogspot.com/p/how-does-gay-
marriage-affect-you-anyway.html
Was Jesus silent on gay "marriage"?
http://www.catholiclane.com/was-jesus-really-silent-on-same-
sex-marriage/
Do the children have a say?
http://littlecatholicbubble.blogspot.com/2013/06/should-
children-sit-down-and-shut-up.html

TRANSGENDERISM

http://www.thepublicdiscourse.com/2016/05/17041/
http://www.thepublicdiscourse.com/2016/06/17166/

PORNOGRAPHY

Help for pornography addiction:
http://catholicmenconquerporn.com/courses/overcome-porn-
addiction
http://www.angelicwarfareconfraternity.org
Internet filter:
http://www.covenanteyes.com/

SCRUPULOSITY

http://scrupulousanonymous.org
*Understanding Scrupulosity: Questions, Helps, and Encourage-
ment,* Rev. Thomas Santa C.Ss.R.

BOOKS FOR CHILDREN

For teaching our younger children how to avoid bad pictures:

Good Pictures Bad Pictures: Porn-Proofing Today's Young Kids,
    Kristen A. Jenson

Sex and reproduction:

The Joyful Mysteries of Life, Catherine and Bernard Scherrer

Wonderfully Made! Babies, Ellen Giangiordano

BOOKS FOR TEENS

Theology of His Body / Theology of Her Body, Jason Evert

General apologetics, good for skeptical teens:

The *Prove It!* books by Amy Welborn

PRAYER AND HOLINESS

The Ordinary Path to Holiness, R. Thomas Richard

*Into Your Hands, Father: Abandoning Ourselves to the God
    Who Loves Us,* Fr. Wilfrid Stinissen

He Leadeth Me, Fr. Walter Ciszek

Trusting God with St. Therese, Connie Rossini

Conversation With Christ, Peter Thomas Rohrbach

IF YOU EVER FEEL LIKE A FAILURE AS A MOTHER

I have felt your pain!

http://littlecatholicbubble.blogspot.com/2011/10/why-i-never-
    should-have-had-eight.html

CONTACT ME

Via my blog, Little Catholic Bubble:

http://littlecatholicbubble.blogspot.com

Via email:

RaisingChasteCatholicMen@gmail.com

Notes

1. Olmsted, Bishop Thomas J. http://intothebreach.org

2. http://www.vatican.va/roman_curia/pontifical_councils/family/documents/rc_pc_family_doc_08121995_human-sexuality_en.html

3. https://www.catholicculture.org/culture/library/dictionary/index.cfm?id=33669

4. Clinton, Hillary, Floor of the US Senate, 2004. https://www.youtube.com/watch?v=6I1-r1YgK9I

5. https://www.gov.uk/how-to-annul-marriage/when-you-can-annul-a-marriage

6. Lowery, Mark. http://www.catholiceducation.org/en/marriage-and-family/sexuality/chastity-before-marriage-a-fresh-perspective.html

7. Spenceley, Arleen. March 13, 2015. http://www.tampabay.com/news/perspective/perspective-how-chastity-can-lead-to-good-sex/2221250

8. Sheen, Fr. Fulton J. "Comments On the Report of The Federal Council of Churches of Christ in America." *The American Birth Control League's Birth Control Review,* Volume XV, Number 4 (April 1931), page 143.

9. Pope Paul VI. http://w2.vatican.va/content/paul-vi/en/encyclicals/documents/hf_p-vi_enc_25071968_humanae-vitae.html

10. *Planned Parenthood of Southeastern Pennsylvania, et al. vs. Robert P. Casey, et al.* Can be found at http://caselaw.findlaw.com/us-supreme-court/505/833.html

11. https://www.reddit.com/r/NoFap/comments/23yg85/ultimate_benefits_thread/ [Warning: contains explicit/offensive

language]

12. Joycelyn Elders, "Abstinence", Penn & Teller: Bullshit! *(Showtime),* 5 June 2006.

13. Flock, Elizabeth. "Devout Catholics Have Better Sex, Study Says." *US News and World Report,* July 17, 2013. http://www.usnews.com/news/articles/2013/07/17/devout-catholics-have-better-sex

14. Suramek, Mae. http://plainjaneactivism.blogspot.com

15. Esolen, Anthony. May 21, 2016. "Remember the Boys" https://www.thecatholicthing.org/2016/05/21/remember-the-boys/

16. Savage, Deborah. "The Nature of Woman in Relation to Man," *Logos* (Winter 2015): 89 & 91.

17. Barack Obama's votes on the "Born-Alive Infants Protection" bills are on the record and searchable. This article includes an overview of his position and audio of an Illinois Senate hearing: http://www.lifenews.com/2012/08/23/new-audio-surfaces-of-obama-defending-infanticide-in-illinois/

18. Jones, Tim. "Barack Obama: Mother not just another girl from Kansas," *Chicago Tribune,* March 27, 2007 http://www.webcitation.org/66cdqjbue

19. https://en.wikipedia.org/wiki/Ann_Dunham

20. http://littlecatholicbubble.blogspot.com/2014/12/my-mother-in-law-carols-conversion.html